Advances in Contemporary Educational Thought Series
Jonas F. Soltis, Editor

INHERITING SHAME
The Story of Eugenics and Racism in America

STEVEN SELDEN

Foreword by
Ashley Montagu

TEACHERS COLLEGE PRESS

Teachers College, Columbia University
New York and London

Published by Teachers College Press, 1234 Amsterdam Avenue, New York, NY 10027

The author gratefully acknowledges the generosity of the journals and publishers cited below that supported the use of this material:

Portions of Chapters 1 and 2 appeared in different form in Selden, S. (1978, November). Eugenics and curriculum: Conservative naturalism in education, 1860–1929. *The Educational Forum*, *XLIII*(1), pp. 67–82.

Portions of Chapter 3 appeared in Selden, S. (1985, Fall). Education policy and biological science: Genetics, eugenics, and the college textbook, c. 1908–1931. *Teachers College Record*, 87, Number 1, pp. 35–52.

Portions of Chapter 4 appeared in Selden, S. (1990). Selective traditions and the science curriculum: Eugenics and the biology textbook, 1914–1949. *Science Education*, 75, 493–512, and Selden, S. (1989). The use of biology to legitimate inequality: The eugenics movement within the high school biology textbook, 1914–1949. In Walter Secada (Ed.), *Equity in Education*, New York: The Falmer Press, pp. 118–145.

Portions of Chapter 5 appeared in Selden, S. (1994, Fall). Early 20th century biological determinism and the classification of exceptional students. In G. Macdonald (Ed.), *Evaluation and Research in Education*. North Somerset: Multilingual Matters, Ltd., and Selden, S. (1983, Spring). Biological determinism and the roots of student classification. *Journal of Education*, 165(2), pp. 175–191.

Portions of Chapter 6 appeared in Selden, S. (1988, Fall). Resistance in school and society: Public and pedagogical debates about eugenics, 1900–1947. *Teachers College Record*, 90(1), pp. 61–84.

Library of Congress Cataloging-in-Publication Data

Selden, Steven.
    Inheriting shame : the story of eugenics and racism in America
/ Steven Selden ; foreword by Ashley Montagu.
    p. cm. — (Advances in contemporary educational thought
series)
  Includes bibliographical references and index.
  ISBN 0-8077-3813-1 (cloth)
  ISBN 0-8077-3812-3 (pbk.)
  1. Eugenics—United States—History. 2. Racism—United
States—History. 3. Eugenics in textbooks. 4. Racism in textbooks.
5. American Eugenics Society—History. 6. United States—Race
relations. I. Title. II. Series.
  HQ755.5.U5 S45 1999
  363.9'2'0973—dc21   98-46778

ISBN 0-8077-3812-3 (paper)
ISBN 0-8077-3813-1 (cloth)

Printed on acid-free paper
Manufactured in the United States of America

06 05 04 03 02 01 00 99   8 7 6 5 4 3 2 1

Contents

Foreword

Professor Selden has asked me to say a few words for his book. It gives me great pleasure to do so, for I have followed his writings with great interest and admiration. In the present work, the culmination of years of cogitation on the experience and meaning of perhaps the most important of all our activities, namely, education, he has accomplished a most important task: the demonstration of the manner in which scientific and pseudo-scientific theories may be used to influence the current and the course of education. Not only that, his book shows clearly how the dead hand of the past may continue to guide the practice of the present as well of the future. This is why I regard Professor Selden's book as of such great importance. Those of us who have spent a considerable part of our lives actively as teachers will not need to be told that something is not quite right about education.

The point I am trying to make is that most of the leading eugenicists of whom Professor Selden writes were the product of our best schools and universities. What happened during their education? Why did they turn out lacking in humanity, compassionless, racist, and in the genetics of their day, impoverished? By the measure of the biological sciences of their time they were ill equipped to evaluate the qualities of others or make recommendations for their control. Indeed, sitting in their citadels of infallibility, in the name of humanity and science they urged on government and the professions the passage of laws of most inhumane and scientifically unsound kind. Professor Selden has dealt with all this admirably in the pages that follow. I would like to recall here the words of H. G. Wells, who in 1922 wrote (the year in which I read them), "History is a race between education and catastrophe." Let us hope that this book furthers our education.

Ashley Montagu
Princeton, New Jersey

Acknowledgments

As my friends, family, and colleagues well know, this volume has been a long time in development. And like all such projects, this one has benefited from having templates of academic excellence available to serve as targets, as well as supportive contexts that allowed the work to be done. That is, knowing where you want to go, while critically important, is insufficient. Making the journey requires more; it requires a helping, caring context if one is to be successful. In that regard I have many to whom I must give thanks. I take full responsibility for this volume's limitations. They are my own. But I also wish to give a full measure of appreciation to those who stayed the course as this book came into being.

While separated by a generation, there are two academics who have served as models for what it means to be an engaged scholar. Speaking consistently and articulately against inappropriate determinist and racist notions of human being, Ashley Montagu and Stephen Jay Gould have served as models for my scholarly endeavors. Their work is exemplary; I hold them blameless for my errors.

Over the years I have also been able to depend on the support of my colleagues in the field of education. To Michael Apple, who first listened to my initial thoughts on this volume I offer deepest thanks. To the late A. Harry Passow, who followed its long trajectory, I offer thanks as well. In addition, I want to thank Daniel Liston, Stephen Fain, James Greenberg, William Foster, Christopher Hartmann, Daniel Margolis, Sharon Fries-Britt, Christopher Giordano, Richelle Patterson, Paul Lombardo, and Alan Stoskopf and friends at Facing History and Ourselves, for their thoughtful reactions to early drafts on the chapters that follow.

Colleagues in the history and philosophy of science have been equally generous with their time and suggestions. To Garland Allen, Hamilton Cravens, Andrew Futterman, Lyndley Darden, Diane Paul, Leo Kamin, Fred Suppe, and David Wasserman, I express my heartfelt appreciation.

For his consistent support, I especially want to thank Jonas Soltis, who combines those rare qualities of being teacher, colleague, and friend. In addition I would like to thank Brian Ellerbeck and Lori Tate of Teachers College Press; Brian allowed me the necessary time to complete the book on my own terms and Lori worked on the manuscript with remarkable thoughtfulness and care.

Decades ago, Susanne K. Langer likened the work of academics to the making of scholarly "mud pies," which were designed to be shared with others in the hope of engendering thoughtful reactions. To my splendid students at the University of Maryland who reacted to my mud pies, I want to publicly offer my words of appreciation. The meaning of this work could never have become clear to its author without their thoughtful and caring analyses. I also want to offer special thanks to Louise Reynolds. Her detailed review of the manuscript offered humane insights that went far beyond her outstanding technical corrections.

Institutions can also serve as supportive contexts to scholarly work. In that regard I want to thank the University of Maryland, whose General Research Board Awards came just at the right times to make this volume a possibility. And to Teachers College, Columbia University, I also want to express my appreciation. Its willingness to enroll me as a graduate student in the late 1960s was surely one of the most important interventions in my life.

To my wife, Pamela, and to my son, Philip, I want to express my love and thanks for their support during the gestation and production of this volume. Scholarship may give meaning to my career. They give meaning to my life.

Lastly, for having shown me that issues of social justice were woven into the fabric of everyday life, I want to thank my late mother and father. As an immigrant and the child of immigrants, their lives spanned the period of time and were shaped by just the issues that are the concern of this volume. They taught me that these issues were important to care about, and the ways in which to care about them. I hope they would be pleased to see what I have done with their lessons. This book is dedicated to their memory.

Series Editor's Introduction

This is a head-shaking book. As Steven Selden tells the story of the eugenics movement in America during the early decades of the twentieth century prior to the holocaust of World War II, every reader's head will turn left and right in rhythmic disbelief. How could prominent Americans publicly voice such racist, anti-Semitic, anti–various ethnic group ideas? As you read the words of the likes of Theodore Roosevelt, Edward Thorndike, Leta Hollingworth, Franklin Bobbitt, Robert Yerkes, G. Stanley Hall, W. W. Charters, Karl Pearson, and others, disbelief escalates. How could they and others advocate such things as institutionalization, segregation, and even sterilization of those with "inferior blood" while promoting selective human breeding of those with "superior blood"? How could this eugenics message of selective breeding and racial betterment become an integral part of high school and college biology texts in the 1920s, 1930s, and 1940s? How could these ideas also penetrate and become part of teacher education during this period?

In this amazing book, Selden answers these questions with the documentation and thoroughness of an able historian while also treating this phenomenon with the moral sensitivity of a social philosopher committed to democratic education. He traces the popularization of ideas about the potential inheritance of such traits as laziness, feeblemindedness, pauperism, alcoholism, criminality, and sexual looseness, as well as intelligence, thrift, honesty, morality, industriousness, and so forth. These were ideas taught to young people in our schools and to their parents at state fairs and in popular magazines.

Selden counters these views with the co-contemporary arguments of some prominent resisters to the basic beliefs of the eugenicists, John Dewey, H. S. Jennings, William Chandler Bagley, and Walter Lippmann. He then describes the advances in modern biology, the discovery of DNA, and the fuller understanding of genetics that brought an end to the simple Mendelian-based eugenicists' view of human inheritance.

His final chapter is a "cautionary tale" regarding contemporary genetics. There are many scientific claims being made today of finding genes that are specifically related to certain human traits, behaviors, and conditions. How should we sort them out? Is the claimed genetic basis for Down

Syndrome and Tay-Sachs disease in the same realm of certainty as claims that there are genes related to criminality, alcoholism, right–left handedness, novelty seeking, or antisocial behavior? Selden treats the contemporary forms of the nature–nurture, inheritance–environment debate with great care and sensitivity. In doing so, he tries to help the reader become more sophisticated or at least more cautious regarding these and future claims of genetic causality.

His message to educators is also clear. Of course there is inheritance. There is also environment and educators can nurture and help individuals develop whatever human potential they are born with by making the learning environment as rich as possible. With Dewey, he recognizes that we can see inheritance as limiting or we can see it as what we or educators have to work with. In a democratic society, Selden argues, the latter is the proper educational posture regarding human potential. His message is a worthy advance of contemporary educational thought about the dialectic of nature and nurture.

Jonas F. Soltis
Series Editor
Advances in Contemporary Educational Thought

Introduction

Humankind's desire to construct an explanation for its varying levels of performance dates back at least to Plato's *Republic*. In that volume, read by a majority of America's undergraduates to this day, Socrates explains that human differences are a reflection of human essences. That is, humanity's behavior is a reflection of the stuff of which it is made. As those essences scale upward in quality from iron and brass through silver to gold, so too do the qualities of the persons of which they are made. While we cannot know how compelling this essentialist argument for human hierarchies and differences was to those ancient Athenian students, we do know that a transformation of that idea gained considerable popularity in the late 19th and early 20th centuries as part of a worldwide movement known as eugenics. Rooted in a deep belief in the overarching importance of heredity in human development, eugenics was described by its twentieth-century supporters as the science of human improvement through programs of controlled breeding. Basing their work on a mix of scientific and pseudo-scientific studies, American Mendelian eugenicists pursued policies of immigration restriction, segregation, and eugenic mating during the first third of this century. Perhaps not surprisingly, many eugenicists, anxious about their social status as well as about immigration-driven demographic changes, saw in eugenics a legitimation of their racial interpretations of differential human worth. Regardless of political disposition however, eugenicists saw the public schools as one important venue for the popularization and dissemination of eugenic policies. This volume traces the links between the hereditarian Popular Eugenics Movement and American education during this century's first three decades.

The late 19th century was a period of revolution in biology. It was a revolution that appeared to reject previously held environmentalist interpretations of human improvement. For example, the work of Jean-Baptiste Lamarck, whose theory that the muscles of blacksmiths would be transmitted to their daughters and sons as "acquired characters" and that had seemed to support environmental reform, was demolished by the research of August Weismann. Weismann had argued by contrast that germ plasm was continuous from generation to generation and was unaffected by environmental change. In addition, the hereditary material had been identified as located in the chromosomes and by the early 1880s Francis Galton had coined the term *eugenics* based on the Greek root meaning "good in birth." Perhaps of greatest significance for the development of the American Eugenics movement was the popularization of the work of Gregor Mendel after its rediscovery in 1900. After the turn of the century this revolution seemed to support American Mendelian eugenicists' belief that a wide variety of human moral, intellectual, and social traits could be easily explained by reference to heredity. In addition to intelligence, this list of heritable traits included patriotism, alcoholism, shiftlessness, pauperism, and a tendency to wander.

There seemed to be implications in these findings for social and educational policy as well. For early 20th century intellectuals who had previously supported environmental reform, it now seemed that heredity was of greatest importance. Human behavior now appeared determined by genetic substrates that were unaffected by the external life of the organism and whose transmission followed fixed laws with mathematical precision. Heredity, many concluded, was of signal importance in predicting human performance and it must play a key role in policies and programs for human betterment. In our contemporary context, this extreme form of hereditary determinism regularly returns, claiming a central place in policymaking (Herrnstein & Murray, 1994; Jensen, 1969, 1981). This book argues that whether in historical or contemporary context, the belief that complex human behavior is determined by genetics is without substantive merit.

The volume that follows builds on the historical analysis of eugenics that began with Ashley Montagu's (1942) ground-breaking analyses of the mythology of biological determinism as well as on contemporary analyses of the eugenics movement (Allen, 1986; Chase, 1977; Cravens, 1978; Gould, 1981; Haller, 1963; Kamin, 1974; Kevles, 1985; Ludmerer, 1972; Rosenberg, 1961). Its purpose is to give meaningful shape to a dimension of the social implications of science that is often left unconsidered. Its purpose is to make sense of the relationship between eugenics and American educational policies and practices during the first three decades of the twentieth century.

This story of the relationship of eugenics to American education makes for a surprising history. It is surprising for its breadth and depth of engagement, and it is surprising for the lack of recognition and understanding that we have of it as practicing educators. While most of us would recognize Edward Thorndike, Leta Hollingworth, and Franklin Bobbitt as having given leadership to educational psychology, gifted education, and curriculum studies respectively, few among us recognize that each of these leaders spoke out in strong support of eugenics. Thorndike and Hollingworth, for example, believed in and popularized eugenics throughout their careers. In addition, we need only scratch the surface of science textbooks published between the wars to find that eugenic content was included in the majority of them as well. It would almost seem as though we have received a selective professional education. That is, we have learned of the technical dimensions of our history (how to make a correlation, how to develop a curricular objective, how to prepare programs for exceptionally gifted students), but we have remained generally unaware of the developers' social policy commitments. I do not wish to commit what my philosophical colleagues would call the "genetic fallacy" here, but in a world that is changing as rapidly as ours in terms of scientific knowledge and social problems, such ignorance of the past is potentially dangerous. Challenges concerning the social achievements of immigrants and those disenfranchised by economic transformations vexed our policy competence in the past. At that time eugenics was seen by many as a possible policy response. As these challenges continue to confront us in the current context, we will need to know more than merely a selection of our professional past if we are not to stumble as similar responses are once again offered.

An active academic Eugenics movement no longer exists in the United States today. The combination of the work of Thomas Hunt Morgan and internal changes in the field of genetics made eugenics unwarranted as science as early as 1915 and the movement was moribund in America by the 1940s. But the idea that humankind is profoundly determined by its heredity has remarkable staying power. Motivated by 20th-century events, by the public's fascination with the "nature–nurture" debate, and by technical changes within genetics, the belief in hereditary determinism returns on a regular basis to play a role in the discourse on public policy. Indeed, whether drawing the attention of its supporters or detractors, hereditarian interpretations of human performance have maintained a continuing place in popular consciousness for more than a century.

The chapters that follow outline the connections between the Popular Eugenics Movement and important American educational practices and policies. The first five chapters focus on eugenics between the early 1900s and the late 1930s. They consider the organization, popularization, program impact, and putative policy implications of Eugenics, as well as resistance to the movement. A sixth chapter analyzes contemporary hereditarian interpretations of complex human behavior and brings the issue of the relationship between human performance and genetic substrates into the current period. Rather than identifying a resurgent eugenics, this chapter urges policymakers to engage in careful analysis and thoughtful caution as they review contemporary behavioral and molecular genetic studies linking complex human behavior and markers.

Chapters 1 and 2 consider the organization and leadership of the American eugenics movement. The chapters focus on eugenically oriented national and international conferences and congresses, as well as on the public policy prescriptions that they developed and supported.

An understanding of the impact of eugenics on American education requires more than evidence of organizational structures alone if one is to be convinced that significant connections existed between eugenics and American education. One needs to know whether eugenics was present in the academic preparation of society's leaders during this period as well. Chapter 3, "Popularizing Eugenics," answers that question by considering the eugenic content presented to college undergraduates in their textbooks during the 1920s and 1930s. In addition, the chapter reviews a series of journals that served to popularize eugenics to the literate public during this period. The eugenicists' concern for influencing public education also focused on teacher training. Once again, the question of evidence is legitimately raised. Did eugenicists attempt to influence the training of prospective teachers during the early twentieth century? This chapter answers this question by reviewing the policy of including eugenics in teacher education programs at the national level during the 1920s.

American eugenicists also recommended using the public schools for the popularization of eugenics. Chapter 4, "Eugenics and the Textbook," looks at one dimension of what we might call the commodified curriculum of the school. It analyzes the eugenic content and policy recommendations of 41 high school biology texts published in the United States between 1914 and 1948.

If eugenics was not to remain peripheral to education policy, it would also have to be supported by educational leaders actively involved in such policy formation. One might legitimately ask whether eugenically committed educators were so involved. Chapter 5, "Biological Determinism and Exceptional Students," reviews the involvement of nationally respected and eugenically committed educational leaders in the development of curricular policies for persons with exceptionalities in the 1920s and 1930s.

Curricular policies and practices are always the consequence of contestation, and one might well ask whether members of the polity resisted eugenics. Chapter 6, "Resisting American Eugenics," identifies scientists, educators, and publicists who carefully articulated resistance to eugenics in their respective professional domains.

In recent years the continuing revolution in molecular genetics and the development of the Human Genome Project have created a public concern for the possibility of a return to the eugenics of the past. Chapter 7, "Human Behavior and Biological Markers: A Cautionary Tale," analyzes a series of research studies that link complex human behavior and markers using chromosomal, DNA, and statistical analyses. The chapter outlines a series of technical and ethical issues raised by these studies and concludes that yesterday's eugenics need not serve as a prologue for tomorrow's genetic policies and programs.

In summary, despite the historically restrictive qualities of many of the policies and programs described in the chapters that follow, it is hoped that the reader will see this volume as optimistic in both tone and purpose. While the story of eugenics and its links to American education is certainly not a positive one, there were policymakers who understood what eugenics was and what it was not. Seeing that it was more ideology than science, they rejected it. Complex human behavior is no more dependent today on genetics than it was in 1903. Human behavior is always the inseparable consequence of potential in context. Education practitioners and policymakers have always been responsible for crafting contexts that maximize the potentialities of our youth. The development of such contexts remain to this day a consuming challenge for those who choose it as their life's work. The history recounted in the following chapters may seem depressing. But it is important for the reader to recognize that eugenics never eliminated our responsibility for developing supportive and caring environments for our students. In many ways the eugenicists' scientifically unjustified arguments only underscored this realization. Offering little compelling scientific data in support of the overriding importance of heredity in shaping complex human behavior, they left us with the task of creating maximally productive environments. That is a splendid challenge and it is a cause for optimism.

INHERITING SHAME
The Story of Eugenics and Racism in America

CHAPTER 1

Organizing American Eugenics: 1903–1921

[The objectives of the Committee on Eugenics are] to investigate and report on heredity in the human race; to devise methods of recording the values of the blood of individuals, families, peoples and races; to emphasize the value of superior blood and the menace to society of inferior blood; and to suggest methods of improving the heredity of the family, the people, or the race.
—David Starr Jordan, Chairman, Committee on Eugenics,
American Breeders Association, 1908

In the early decades of the 20th century, the assumptions that race and heredity were central to human development and social progress were basic components of American social thought. The belief that heredity was the primary factor in determining human betterment was a core assumption of the scientific, social, and political movement known as Eugenics. The Eugenics movement argued that if humankind were to improve, the parents of future generations would have to be carefully selected. To fulfill this goal, eugenicists supported policies of immigration restriction, segregation of those judged socially "unfit," and programs of human selective breeding. Supported by a broad spectrum of American intellectuals, the Eugenics movement influenced decisions of the courts on sterilization policy, made itself present in the school and college curriculum, and often found common ground with American race thinkers and nativists. While eugenics would come to mean many things to its followers, the commitment to the overarching importance of heredity and to the improvement of humankind through hereditary manipulation remained common to all of its adherents. As a consequence, the American Popular Eugenics Movement was the intellectual home for biological determinist thinking in the early decades of the 20th century. In contrast to the optimism reflected in the American character of the early 19th century, eugenicists were profoundly anxious when confronted with America's increasing social diversity in the early 20th century. While eugenics certainly found a rich medium for growth in America, the movement was initially an import from Great Britain.

American Eugenics had its roots in Britain, where Francis Galton developed the term in the early 1880s. Galton, a man of catholic interests, had observed that the leaders of British society were far more likely to be related to each other than chance alone might allow. From a range of possible explanations for this phenomenon, Galton drew a hereditarian interpretation. Believing that the superior heredity of the British ruling class preordained its leadership positions, he proposed a program of selective breeding in the 1860s (Cowan, 1969) and by 1883 he had coined the term *eugenics* (Galton, 1883, p. 24).

By the late 1890s, eugenics had crossed the Atlantic and gained popularity with educated Americans who were concerned for what they saw as threats to the "American stock." Industrialization and immigration were rapidly transforming American society. This transformation from an agrarian to an urban-industrial order, with its attendant challenges of dependency, delinquency, and pauperism, had become a source of national anxiety (Rosenberg, 1974). With "influential voices [calling] for custodial care, restriction of marriage, and sterilization," eugenics offered a solution consistent with Progressivism's hereditarian strand (Haller, 1963, p. 57; see also Persons, 1958). Eugenics, particularly with a Mendelian turn, would prove to be the catalyst that would fuse these economic, demographic, and psychological anxieties into a "crusade" that would continue from the turn of the century into the 1940s (Haller, 1963, p. 57).

If the late 19th century was a period of revolution in American society, it was also a period of revolution in biology. In its European context, this revolution would lead to the rejection of environmental policies for human improvement (Cravens, 1978, p. 17). Environmental reform, it seemed, could have no lasting effect on following generations. If one really wanted to improve future generations the hereditarians concluded, one must control their germ plasm.

Of greatest significance for the development of American Eugenics was the rediscovery, in 1900, of the research of the Moravian monk Gregor Mendel. Mendel had undertaken a series of breeding experiments with a particular variety of the pea plant in the 1860s. He found that when he cross-fertilized the plants, particular traits were transmitted to future generations in predictable mathematical ratios. For example, when he crossed pure-bred plants, plants that always presented a single trait, wrinkled texture was always dominant over smooth. Since there was no commonly accepted term for the genetic material prior to 1909 (in fact, the term *genetics* itself was not coined until 1906), and having no clear understanding of what we today would call the gene, Mendel used the term element ("Elemente") to refer to the substrate that was transmitted from generation to generation (Mayr, 1982, pp. 716, 736). He theorized that purebred peas had received two identical elements for texture from their parent generation. When these wrinkled and smooth peas were cross-fertilized, the next generation of peas were all wrinkled, though these wrinkled peas contained elements for smooth texture. The wrinkled trait was dominant. It was when Mendel crossed these hybrids, each of which contained one dominant and one recessive element, that nature's mathematical elegance appeared to reveal itself. In every case, the first hybrid crosses produced a ratio of 3:1 in favor of wrinkled peas. By the turn of the century, the work of Weismann and Mendel had given strong support to American hereditarians and their social theories. As Cravens points out:

> The rising reputation of the new germ plasm, brought inheritance to the forefront of professional biology's literature in the early twentieth century. Many biologists wrote as if for each trait there existed a determiner in the germ plasm; environment was of negligible importance because acquired characters could not be inherited; the determiners were "unit characters" and were inherited and varied according to the famous Mendelian ratios. (Cravens, 1978, p. 41)

Even though it would soon become evident that their position was without strong scientific justification, American Mendelian eugenicists naively applied Mendel's notions to all complex human traits. They argued that moral, intellectual, and social qualities could be easily explained by reference to the workings of heredity.

For American eugenicists, there were implications in these findings for social and educational policy as well. Many early 20th century intellectuals who had previously assumed that changes in environment were required for social reform now focused on heredity as the primary agent for bringing about social change. Human behavioral traits appeared to be determined by genetic substrates that were unaffected by the external life of the organism. Heredity, many concluded, was of signal importance in predicting human performance and it must play a key role in policies and programs for human betterment.

In our contemporary context, this extreme form of hereditary determinism regularly returns, claiming a central place in policy making (Herrnstein & Murray, 1994; Jensen, 1969, 1981). While science and history have shown that the basis for these claims is without substantive merit, this resistance and recognition would not begin until after 1915. And so, if we were to return to the early 20th century, we would find that in addition to being quite popular, American eugenics was also very well organized.

During the first three decades of the 20th century, hereditarian thought in the United States was aggressively integrated into a series of organizations committed to eugenics. This chapter will focus on the leadership,

structure, and public policy prescriptions of a number of those organizations as they were developed in their annual meetings. While we review
their policies for differential birth rates, immigration restriction, and sterilization, we will consider the role they believed eugenics would play in
legitimating a vision of human improvement through hereditary manipulation. As we shall see in following chapters, it would be a role that would
encompass both educational policies and the content of the curriculum.

Directed by a limited number of extreme hereditarians, organizations
committed to eugenics increased in both number and size between 1903
and 1932. One of the first to actively pursue a eugenical public policy program was the American Breeders Association.

THE AMERICAN BREEDERS ASSOCIATION (1903)

The history of American Eugenics can be traced to the founding of the
Carnegie Institution in Washington, DC, to the formation of the American
Breeders Association (ABA) in 1903, and to the person of Charles Benedict
Davenport (Figure 1.1). A committed Mendelian eugenicist, Davenport
believed that human traits such as laziness, wanderlust, and pauperism
were heritable and that their patterns of transmission were in need of research. After successfully petitioning the Carnegie Institution for $34,250
for the formation and continuance of the Station for the Experimental Study
of Evolution in Cold Spring Harbor, New York, in 1903, he took a leadership role in the American Breeders Association.

Gathering like-minded individuals about him, the newly appointed
director of the association's Eugenics Section helped to organize a series
of research committees and in 1906 formed the Committee on Eugenics to
"investigate and report on heredity in the human race, and emphasize the
value of superior blood and the menace to society of inferior blood" (Dunn,
1951, pp. 60–65). Additional ABA committees focused on the Heritability
of Feeblemindedness; Insanity; Epilepsy; Criminality; Deaf-Mutism; Eye
Defects; Genealogy; the Inheritance of Mental Traits; Immigration; and
Sterilization and Other Means of Eliminating Defective Germ Plasm. For
Davenport, a nativist who took pride in his Puritan roots, the threat of inferior blood had personal meaning and he warned that "the best of the
grand old New England stock [was] dying out through a failure to repro-
duce" (quoted in Haller, 1963, pp. 62–63). With committee members including Henry Fairfield Osborn, president of the American Museum of
Natural History; Roswell Johnson, co-author of the best-selling college textbook *Applied Eugenics* (1918); Luther Burbank, the plant breeder; Alexander
Graham Bell, world-famous inventor; and President David Starr Jordan and

FIGURE 1.1. Charles Benedict Davenport, Director of the American Breeders Association's Eugenics Section. Courtesy of the American Philosophical Society, Philadelphia.

Professor Vernon L. Kellogg of Leyland Stanford University, the membership represented a virtual "interlocking directorate" of American Eugenics. This leadership cadre would continue to lead organized American Eugenics throughout the 1920s and 1930s.

Organized American Eugenics could not have achieved its successes without Charles Davenport's remarkable organizational skills. As an early and respected scholar in genetics, he was one of the first to bring Karl Pearson's biometrical studies to the attention of American geneticists and his Carnegie-funded Station for Experimental Evolution was considered a prestigious research institution (Allen, 1986, p. 235). But his interests were to change from biometrics to an extreme form of Mendelism, and by the end of the decade this change would distort his career.

By 1910 he had found a sympathetic listener and generous sponsor for this eugenic research in the person of Mrs. E. H. Harriman. Over the next 8 years she funded the Eugenics Record Office as a "center for research in human genetics and for propaganda in eugenics" (Haller, 1963, p. 64). From this institutional base, Davenport devoted his considerable intellect and energy to the popularization of the credo he would later refer to as the "religion of eugenics." Along with this religious conviction he took the extreme view that the inheritance of all human traits followed simple Mendelian ratios and would be easy to control through breeding programs. As Haller notes, Davenport was

> a pioneer in the study of human genetics. . . . He had the facilities and support to create a world center for painstaking and important investigations in the heredity of man. That he did not do so was a tragedy resulting largely from his own scientific methods and temperament. (Haller, 1963, p. 66)

The tragedy however was not for Davenport alone. For those segregated and sterilized in America, and for those trapped in Europe before the juggernaut of World War II by distorted Mendelian interpretations of human capacities, the tragedy was terminal. With lives more tragic than Davenport's, they were separated, neutered, and eliminated, in keeping with policies he advocated throughout his professional career.

In 1911, during his second year as director of the Eugenics Record Office, Davenport published *Heredity in Relation to Eugenics*. Cited by more than one-third of the high school biology textbooks used between the wars, *Heredity in Relation to Eugenics* tied fears of social chaos to the themes of race and differential immigration. Linking types of behaviors to types of persons, he outlined a bimodal distribution of antisocial behaviors and immigrants. "The population of the United States," he warned,

> will, on account of the recent influx of immigrants from Southeastern Europe, rapidly become darker in pigmentation, smaller in stature, more mercurial, more attached to music and art, more given to crimes of larceny, kidnapping, assault, murder, rape, and sex-immorality and less given to burglary, drunkenness, and vagrancy than were the original English settlers. (p. 219)

One year after these comments on the differential worth of immigrants, Davenport returned to the land of his ancestors and attended the First International Congress of Eugenics.

However, not all in attendance were in agreement with Davenport's extreme Mendelian views. For example, Harvard's R. C. Punnett (1912) (who would debunk the scientific legitimacy of programs of negative eugenics within the decade) cautioned, "except in very few cases our knowledge of heredity in man is . . . far too slight and too uncertain to base legislation upon. In addition," he cautioned,

> experience derived from plants and animals has shewn that problems of considerable complexity can be unraveled by the experimental method, and the characters concerned brought under control. Though the direct method is

hardly feasible in man, much may be learnt by collecting accurate pedigrees. . . . But it must be clearly recognized that the collection of such pedigrees is an arduous undertaking demanding high critical ability, and only to be carried out satisfactorily by those who have been trained in and are alive to the trend of genetic research. (p. 138)

As we shall see in a future chapter concerning H. H. Goddard's assistants at the Vineland Training School, too few of Punnett's caveats were considered as organized Eugenics gained strength across the Atlantic.

Appropriate to an age that saw itself as progressive, eugenicists searched for scientific solutions that could order the disarray they saw in an urban corporate America impacted by a large immigrant population. The Progressive Era can be seen as under the influence of what Stow Persons (1958) identifies as the Naturalistic Mind, which had "a particular veneration for scientific fact as the most accurate, dependable, and valuable form of knowledge available to [humankind]" (pp. 222–223). While some during this period might have been comfortable with notions of differential racial worth, a belief in naturalism did not preordain one to support racism or nativism. While the members of race-betterment organizations were often powerful, and in many cases patrician members of society, they varied in their social and political commitments and prescriptions. "Consistency of outlook was not one of [the Naturalists'] virtues. Among their ranks were to be found optimists and pessimists, determinists and believers in free agency, democrats and authoritarians, humanists and theists" (Persons, 1958, p. 222). True enough. But naturalists of a determinist and authoritarian strain would prove to be the lead actors in eugenic organizations as they continued to organize around issues of social and educational policy (Selden, 1988a).

FIRST NATIONAL CONFERENCE ON RACE BETTERMENT (1914)

The First National Conference on Race Betterment was held in Battle Creek, Michigan, in 1914 and it drew the attention and participation of many of those 20th-century naturalists. Once again, the conferees came from various places on what might be called the nature–nurture spectrum. The participants included the liberal social worker Jacob Riis, the conservative supporter of immigration restriction Robert DeCourcy Ward, and the moderate social evolutionist and president of the Tuskegee Institute Booker T. Washington.

Riis (1914), whose photographs of New York City slum life helped change the very shape of tenement buildings, spoke out in favor of environmental reform. "We have heard friends here talk about heredity. The word has run in my ears until I am sick of it," he complained to his listeners. "There is just one heredity in all the world that is ours—we are all children of God, and there is nothing in the whole big world that we can do in His service without it." Pointing to the environmental causes of youthful delinquency, he continued, "there are, dear friends, not any who are deliberately bad, but plenty whom we make bad" (pp. 243–245).

By contrast, the nativist Robert DeCourcy Ward's presentation appears almost in direct reaction to Riis's argument. In his speech, "Race Betterment and Our Immigration Laws," Ward (1914) focused on the degenerative effects of immigration and strongly recommended "proper eugenic selection of the incoming alien millions. Let us see to it," he demanded, "that we are protected, not merely from the burden of supporting alien defectives, but from that 'watering down of the nation's blood' which results from their reproducing their own kind after admission" (p. 546). Placing himself squarely with the extreme hereditarians, Ward quoted the British eugenicist Karl Pearson to the effect that "you cannot change the leopard's spots and you cannot change good stock to bad. You may dilute it, possibly spread it over a wide area, spoiling the good stock, but until it ceases to multiply, it will not cease to be" (p. 546). A review of these competing papers strongly suggests that the concept of race betterment was a broad one and that the nature–nurture debate was alive and well in Battle Creek in the fall of 1914.

Another speaker at the conference, and one who surely would have realized that Pearson's goals for halting population growth could also be achieved by lynchings and burnings, was Booker T. Washington (1914). Speaking out in protest against a misreading of hereditarian data as well as in defense of people of color, Washington explained that African Americans "are worth saving, are worth making a strong, helpful part of the American body politic." Continuing in a tone that was more than a bit ironic, he pointed out that after hundreds of years African Americans were still a presence on the North American continent, explaining that "this is not an easy thing for any dark skinned race to do when it is near you." Further, he observed, "the American negro is practically the only race with a dark skin that has ever undergone the test of living by the side of the Anglo-saxon, looking him in the face and really surviving" (p. 412). Washington's bitter humor notwithstanding, his request to the conference participants was plain enough. If the American Negro was to become a fully integrated member of the American society, changes would be needed. And these changes would have to be environmental.

The tension between euthenics, or environmental reform, and eugenics was also reflected in the posters displayed at the conference. One poster identified the causes of degeneracy as including heredity and an unnatural and unwholesome environment, while another recommended simple, natural habits of life and abstinence from drugs, and that marriages be eugenically planned. This call for environmental and hereditary improvement was also one of the major themes in John H. Kellogg's Presidential Address, which recommended prizes for the "finest families and the best health and endurance records" as well as for the creation of a "Eugenics Registry Office . . . to establish a race of human thoroughbreds" (Kellogg, 1914, p. 447).

It is worth noting that the conference represented complex reactions to human improvement and not everyone shared President Kellogg's human-capital goals nor his equestrian ideals. One participant went so far as to question the "cocksureness [of the] unjustifiable conclusions which the eugenicists had drawn. The vogue of these conclusions," the psychologist Adolphus Miller (1914) continued, was "likely to delay progress by putting our thinking back twenty years" (p. 465). His point was that eugenicists had made the reductive error made by many Naturalists; they had erred by reducing social problems to biological causes. "The[se] social problems," Miller concluded, "have nothing whatever to do with biological inheritance" (p. 470). While these caveats were voiced at the conference, they represented a minority position.

The majority position was well represented by the social theorist Herbert Spencer, whose words appear on the proceedings' title page. "To be a good animal," Spencer charged, "is the first requisite to success in life, and to be a Nation of good animals is the first condition of national prosperity" (Spencer, 1914). What was troubling about the implications of Spencer's position on human capital development in 1914 is equally troubling today. While such policies tend to speak to the development of human capital, they include scant discussion of reciprocal responsibilities to human labor. More specifically, in Spencer's argument, human capital is rationalized in terms of a productive state. Missing in 1914, and in many contemporary policy formulations, is a discussion of a just distribution of material as well as intellectual capital in the face of increasing global competition and social inequities.

SECOND NATIONAL RACE BETTERMENT CONFERENCE (1915)

One year after Spencer's words directed the conferees to focus on issues of national biological strength and economic development, the Race Betterment Foundation held its second national conference. In slightly less assertive and slightly more anxious terms than those of Spencer, the 1915 conference proposed to "assemble and discuss the evidence of race deterioration and to promote race betterment" (Race Betterment Foundation, 1915, title page). While considerably shorter than those of the 1914 conference—the 1915 proceedings numbered only 160 pages as compared with the earlier conference's 625—the proceedings still contained a number of provocative speeches.

One such address was presented by Paul Popenoe (1915), whose work exemplifies the way in which hereditarian beliefs can become destructive to the interests of society's poor. His paper, "Natural Selection in Man," offers ample evidence that he knew that it was Spencer and not Darwin who fathered the phrase "survival of the fittest." In his discussion of infant mortality rates, he cautions that his audience "not lay too much stress upon the word 'environment'" (p. 56). High infant mortality rates were not a cause for alarm. Indeed, quite the contrary was true. In Popenoe's view those rates of illness and death exemplified natural selection at work. Did high rates of infant mortality among those living in unsanitary and overcrowded urban slums require environmental reform? Not in Popenoe's view. After all, he explained, "infant mortality does effect a 'weeding out' of the unfit" (Popenoe, 1915, p. 56).

FIGURE 1.2. Roswell Johnson, co-author with Paul Popenoe of *Applied Eugenics*, 1922. Courtesy of the American Philosophical Society, Philadelphia.

Popenoe's (1915) grisly optimism was applied to tuberculosis mortality rates among the poor as well. In a remarkable example of logical gymnastics, he allowed that the tuberculosis bacillus does not cause death. Contrary to popular belief, his own studies of "overcrowding, bad sanitation, [and] poor food commonly said to be at the root of the white plague, [had found] this correlation to be insignificant" (p. 56). We may wonder what the cause of tuberculosis-related mortality was if it was not to be found in the bacterium itself? Popenoe's answer was simple and direct: Tuberculosis mortality was due to poor heredity. Those who died of the disease did so because they inherited low resistance to it. Using the eugenicists' hereditarian argument, he concluded:

> Science knows no way to make good breeding stock out of bad, and the future of the race is determined by the kind of children which are born and survive to become parents in each generation. There are only two ways to improve the germinal character of the race, to better it in a fundamental and enduring manner. One is to kill off the weaklings born in each generation. That is Nature's way, the old method of natural selection which we all agreed must be supplanted. When we abandon that, we have but one conceivable alternative, and that is to adopt some means by which fewer weaklings will be born in each generation. The only hope for permanent race betterment under social control is to substitute a selective birth-rate for Nature's selective death-rate. That means—eugenics. (p. 61)

I have included this rather long quotation due to the clarity with which Popenoe presents these determinist ideas, and because in 3 years' time these same themes would find their way into his very popular college textbook, *Applied Eugenics*, co-authored with Roswell Johnson (Figure 1.2). As we shall see in later chapters, it was in ways such as these that the organizers of American Eugenics would move their extreme hereditarian views from the conference floor to the curriculum and then to the classroom.

Differential birthrates were a central issue for eugenical organizations and Harvard's Irving Fisher (1915) was quite willing to recommend programs of sterilization for the intellectually challenged: "Gentlemen and ladies," he greeted the Battle Creek audience, "you have no idea . . . how rapidly we could exterminate . . . [Cretinism] if we really got at it" (p. 68). On the positive side of the eugenical equation, J. H. Kellogg (1915) was also ready to "get at it" and he once again called for a Eugenics Registry. Citing Gregor Mendel and Luther Burbank, he made the remarkable promise of the creation of "a new species of man . . . in not more than six generations" (p. 87).

As noted earlier, Race Betterment conferees were a diverse lot and Kellogg was willing to temper his recommendation with the admission that in his process of creation, both environmental and hereditary manipulation would be required. But for those who believed in the overriding importance of heredity, a different organization must have appeared a necessity, and Davenport and others were more than willing to satisfy this demand.

In the early 20th century, Battle Creek, Michigan, had become an organizational center for the complex movement for human improvement in the United States. When the Race Betterment Foundation participated in the 50th anniversary celebration of the Battle Creek Sanitarium in 1916, the peripatetic Davenport was once again on the program. Linking eugenics, immigration, and the state, he spoke on "Eugenics as Religion." "Eugenics has to do with racial development," he explained, and "it accepts the fact of differences in people—physical differences, mental differences, differences in emotional control" (quoted in Chase, 1977, pp. 161–162). While these differences might have been a source of delight to Charles Darwin, they offered no encouragement to Davenport. Rather than seeing difference as a starting point for the development of an individual's potential, Davenport presented difference as exemplifying how little one could do in the face of a seemingly deterministic heredity. Eugenics, as he explained it, was "based upon the principle that nothing can take the place of innate qualities. While it recognizes the value of culture it insists that culture of a trait is futile, where the germs of the trait are absent" (Chase, 1977, p. 162). To this dour interpretation of human possibility, Davenport added his eugenical creed:

> I believe in striving to raise the human race and more particularly our nation and community to the highest place of social organization, of cooperative work, and of effective endeavor. . . . I believe that I am the trustee of the germ plasm that I carry . . . and that I betray the trust if (the germ plasm being good) I so act as to jeopardize it. . . . I believe that, having made our choice in marriage carefully, we, the married pair, should seek to have 4 to 6 children. . . . I believe in such a selection of immigrants as shall not tend to adulterate our national germ plasm with socially unfit traits. . . . I believe in doing it for the race. (quoted in Steggerda, 1944, p. 7)

Given this credo, the reader may not be surprised to find that Davenport was selected by the National Research Council to study the physical dimensions of Army recruits "as a way to discover the 'weak germ plasm' among immigrants, and therefore protect American culture from disorder" (Cravens, 1978, p. 115). With this authoritarian framing of the issues of chaos and order during this century's second decade, Davenport went on to become active in the Galton Society. That society would prove to be yet another organization placing the needs of race and state above those of the individual.

THE GALTON SOCIETY (1918)

Organized American race betterment took many forms. In its most destructive incarnation it became racism with its "most prominent element . . . [being] the scientific study of racial differences according to the principles of physical anthropology" (Persons, 1958, p. 277). In *The Triumph of Evolution* (1978), his outstanding volume outlining the history of the nature–nurture controversy, Hamilton Cravens ties the beginnings of the nature–nurture debate to cultural anthropology's rejection of racism and to the person of Robert H. Lowie. As a student of Franz Boas and a curator at the American Museum of Natural History, Lowie delivered a series of lectures in 1917 in which he rejected the biological determinism of the physical anthropologists of his day. Cravens (1978) marks the date of his lectures as the beginning of the heredity-environment controversy, noting that "the culture idea was at odds with the notion of 'Nordic' superiority" (pp. 90–92).

In 1918 then, partly as a rejection of Boasian cultural anthropology and partly from a desire to propagandize for racial and political ends, the Galton Society was formed in New York City. Named for the father of eugenics, Sir Francis Galton, the society was interested from its very inception in the racial differentiation of human qualities. Joining already chartered members Davenport, Grant, and Osborn were Princeton biologist E. G. Conklin; Yale geographer Ellsworth Huntington; Carnegie Institution President John C. Merriam; Columbia University Zoologist William Gregory; J. Howard MacGregor; and the leader of American educational measurement, Teachers College's Edward Lee Thorndike. To these names, which come from the Henry Fairfield Osborn Papers at the American Museum of Natural History, Haller (1963) also adds the racist Lathrop Stoddard, F. A. Woods, E. A. Hooton, and Raymond Pearl (p. 73).

The society's racial animus was articulated by the anti-Semite Grant when he wrote to Osborn describing the organization as

> an anthropological society (or somatological society as you call it) here in New York City with a central governing body, self elected and self perpetuating, and very limited in numbers, and also confined to native Americans, who are anthropologically, socially, and physically sound, no Bolsheviki need apply. (quoted in Chase, 1977, p. 165)

Grant wanted both the Galton Society and the Galtonian society that it would create to be alike. They were to be for the ideologically, physically, and racially pure. He planned to achieve these ends by joining physical anthropology and eugenics.

Organizations such as the Galton Society also joined their hereditarian ideas to American nativism. As the new science of genetics was applied to problems in agriculture, eugenicists attempted to capture and apply them to policies for controlled human procreation.

In planning their eugenic social order, Galton's 20th-century followers had to confront the issue of the criteria for permissible marriage partners. While they might have selected future parents from the whole of America's outstanding citizens, this approach was fraught with difficulties. For America, then as now, was a racially and ethnically diverse society and an open competition might easily find members from any of these groups listed among the nation's best. This would have been anathema to the Galton Society. If the society, as an organization, was to keep Southern and Eastern European immigrants and Americans of color out of the pool, then an alternative approach would be required. The society's solution was to initiate a program of selection using measures of differential ability by race. To undertake a program for the identification of such differences in culturally bounded areas such as intellect, morality, and beauty would be eugenic in a sense, but it would be something more: It would be racist. The plan and the organization were both racist. This may be best understood through an analysis of the membership and programs of the Galton Society itself.

In April 1919, Professor William Gregory submitted a list of potential Fellows for the Galton Society Laboratory Committee to Henry Fairfield Osborn (Gregory, 1919). The list supplies not only the names of those candidates but also the reasons for their nomination. These reasons are very useful in understanding the organization's intentions vis-à-vis race and achievement. Included on the list was Columbia University psychologist Robert S. Woodworth, who was identified as giving "particular attention to the psychological differences of races" (Gregory, 1919). Another potential fellow was Professor A. E. Jenks of the Anthropology Department of the University of Minnesota; Jenks was working on the effects of race mixing. The list also included Professor Robert M. Yerkes. Yerkes's name is familiar to today's student of educational psychology due to his active involvement in developing the Army Alpha and Beta tests for use during the First World War. Yerkes was also the president of the American Psychological Association.

Three years prior to his nomination, Yerkes had the opportunity to address the National Education Association (NEA) on issues of psychological and sociological importance. In this speech he called for an intensive study of a single school system for a period of 10 or 20 years. He reasoned that much could be learned from such a long-term activity "concerning the nature of the children who later became social blights or social blessings—

paupers, criminals, mental dependents, the insane, inventors, artists, reformers, leaders in various walks of life" (Yerkes, 1916, p. 251). Some who heard his talk may have assumed that he was searching for environmental correlates for the trajectories of those lives—that he was searching for ways to intervene in the social contexts of those young people in order to improve their chances for social success. I believe that such an environmental interpretation would be wrong. It is far more likely that Yerkes was selected by the Galton Society due to his hereditarian interpretation of the causes for those various life outcomes. As Gregory (1922) noted, Yerkes' work dealt with the "relative efficiency of different groups of men in the army [and will] . . . very likely make the relative values of racial groups a subject for further investigation." Cross-cultural studies of the history of psychology suggest that eugenics had a similar impact in the United Kingdom. Reflecting on the roots of statistically oriented research in Great Britain, Torsten Husen (1984) notes that "what strikes the student of educational research . . . is the heavy impact of the Galtonian tradition with its focus on individual differences" (p. 6). Undergirded as they were by social theory as well as science, Husen points out that "group intelligence testing was motivated by the eugenics movement and by Galton" (p. 6). Eugenics did not make this world, but it did assist greatly in its rationalization and Yerkes was a central player in that process.

Another popularizer of eugenics during that period was the notorious racist Lathrop Stoddard. Stoddard, who authored *The Rising Tide of Color Against White Supremacy*, "detested the new immigration, . . . worshipped the Nordic, [and feared for the] mongrelization and destruction of civilization" (Haller, 1963, p. 49). Gregory's list included his name as well. Such were the nominees for fellowships in the Galton Society Laboratory Committee.

Disregarding their intentions for the moment, I believe that the nominees were selected on the grounds that they were perceived as researching human performance distinctions in terms of race. Recalling Madison Grant's earlier racial and ethnic limits on membership, we may conclude that Woodworth was nominated for researching psychological differences by race; that Jenks was nominated in the hope that he would uncover negative consequences from race mixing; that Yerkes was nominated for his support for racial hierarchies; and that Lathrop Stoddard was nominated for his general position that the white race was threatened with disintegration. This list of nominees suggests that the Galton Society viewed eugenics as useful not just for the creation of a meritocratic state, but for the rationalization of a racist order. It is important to recognize that while its membership was limited, this was not a marginal organization. The society's members played important roles in American education in the years following 1918, and a more careful consideration of its meetings may help us to see how these links were forged.

An organizational commitment to race differences can be found in the topics discussed at Galton Society meetings. In late 1922 or early 1923, for example, Drs. Carl Brigham and Robert Yerkes were scheduled to present a paper to the society on the racial aspects of intelligence tests (Gregory, letter dated October 11, 1922). There is little doubt that they were speaking on Brigham's soon-to-be published findings from *A Study of American Intelligence* (1923). Yerkes had written the introduction to the book and had played a key role in the development of the tests. It was the Army test scores Brigham had analyzed.

For those today who are unfamiliar with the volume, its findings helped to legitimate a belief in the differential intelligence between Anglo and African Americans in the 1920s. Brigham even went so far as to acknowledge that his extreme treatment of the race hypothesis was informed by Ripley's *Races of Europe* and Madison Grant's *The Passing of the Great Race* (1921). Based primarily on the data from the Army tests, Brigham's (1923) conclusions spoke to differential intelligence by race, to a hierarchy of racial worth, to the need for stringent immigration restriction, and to the threat posed to America by indivduals of African inheritance. In concluding his work, he spoke out against democracy in a way that must have been well received by many of the socially anxious members of the Galton Society: "In a definite way," he explained,

> the results which we obtain by interpreting the army test data by the race hypothesis support Mr. Madison Grant's thesis of the superiority of the Nordic Type: "The Nordics are, all over the world, a race of soldiers, sailors, adventurers, and explorers, but above all, of rulers, organizers, and aristocrats in sharp contrast to the essentially peasant and democratic character of the Alpines." (p. 182)

Brigham's work also supported the society's aversion to racial or ethnic intermarriage. "We must now frankly admit," he cautioned his readers, that undesirable results "would ensue from a cross between the Nordic in this country with the Alpine Slav, with the degenerated hybrid Mediterranean, or with the negro" (p. 208). In light of these comments it isn't difficult to envision the people Brigham had in mind when he warned that one must look "toward the prevention of the continued propagation of defective strains in the present population" (p. 210). The policies Brigham outlined to his readers in 1923 are eerily like those of Germany in 1933. He argued that a well-organized and efficient society must reflect a hierarchy of races with the Nordic at its acme; that racial intermarriage would lead to undesirable results; and that in the event that such a union should occur, the best course of action was sterilization.

The consequences of intermarriage were also of considerable concern to Davenport, whose problematic research led him to conclude that hybridization of a people made them dissatisfied, restless, and ineffective (in Haller, 1963, p. 148). In December 1928, he spoke before the society on "The Evidence of Disharmony in Negro-White Crosses" (Osborn, 1928). It is troubling to realize that in the decade before the National Socialists took power in Germany, both Brigham and Davenport had foreshadowed their programs in speeches delivered before the Galton Society in the United States. Indeed, many members of the Galton Society would look to Germany in the 1930s as a positive example of these very social policies in action.

It is important that we do not miss the complexity of this history as we review it. We need to take care that we do not use today's perspectives to freeze those eugenic actors into historical grotesques. Individuals reconsidered their positions and changed their minds. This was certainly true in the case of Brigham. While he aligned himself with race thinkers, white supremacists, and immigration restrictionists in 1923, he did in time revise his position. Writing in 1930 on the conclusions that he drew from immigrant group intelligence test data, he totally disavowed his earlier positions as unjustified. He painfully reported that

> this review has summarized some of the more recent test findings which show that comparative studies of various national and racial groups may not be made with existing tests, and which show, in particular, that one of the most pretentious of these comparative racial studies—the writer's own—was without foundation. (Brigham, 1930, p. 165)

As Brigham's position changed, so, too, did William Gregory's interpretation of the Galton Society. In 1930, Gregory offered to resign from the society after recognizing his primary interest—"the evolution of primates"—and the interests of Grant and Osborn as substantively different. "At the time I was made a charter member of the Galton Society," he wrote to Grant, "I was really very ignorant of the issues in which you and Professor Osborn were especially interested, namely the physical differences between human races and the social values of their mental and moral traits" (Gregory, 1930). It may be that men such as Gregory, who had been instrumental in legitimating notions of racial hierarchies in public discourse, can be seen as some of the first to lead the movement for its rejection. But it should be noted that as late as 1931, both Brigham and Yerkes were still listed as members of the Advisory Council of the American Eugenics Society (*Eugenics*, 1931, December).

In concluding our discussion of the Galton Society it is useful to consider the provocative work of the late sociologist Donald MacKenzie (1981). MacKenzie suggests that the American Galtonians' success was due in part to their lack of turf battles. For example, in the British context, an acrimonious debate developed between supporters of Mendelism, on the one hand, and of biometrics on the other (Provine, 1971). The biometricians looked at external differences between individuals, for example variations in height; they did not believe that Mendel's work in internal elements was important for understanding evolutionary change. However, neither Thorndike nor Yerkes was a biologist, and they were quite successful in working together for eugenic ends. This lack of ideological hair-splitting on the part of the Galton Society members permitted them to advance policies that served their class and race interests. Perhaps in the context of post–World War I America, where access to wealth and social position was differentially distributed by class and race, it was sufficient to measure the symptoms of inequality and identify them as the disease itself. After all, poor immigrants would surely do less well on measures of intelligence and health than their indigenous Anglo counterparts. Viewing these differences as though they were innate and immutable was all that the members of the society needed to do to serve their own positions.

THE SECOND INTERNATIONAL
CONGRESS OF EUGENICS (1921)

Eugenics had become a worldwide movement by the time the Second International Congress of Eugenics was scheduled for the American Museum of Natural History in September 1921. With its planning committees heavily involved in the leadership of both the Race Betterment Foundation and the Galton Society, the congress claimed an attendance in excess of 300 with an active membership of more than 365.

Whether they were held in Battle Creek, London, or New York, the proceedings regularly included various poster sessions and exhibits reflecting the membership's continuing concern for differential racial worth and fecundity. Charts displayed at the 1921 congress classified paupers as unfit and compared the increasing differential between the growth rates of recent immigrants and Northern European stock. The clear policy implication was that pauperism was a heritable trait open to programs of selective breeding: Increase Northern European fecundity and control the procreation of the poor.

One particularly ghoulish exhibit used terms of physical anthropology that Madison Grant would have admired: to compare Negro and white fetuses. Recreated in plaster of Paris, their prenatal expressions set for eternity, these fetuses surrendered their physical measurements to the cause of racial differentiation. "The first toe is the longest in a greater percentage of white than negro fetuses," the text explained, and "in the latter race the heel is more prominent than in the white." After analyzing 455 white and 168 Negro fetuses, the researcher, Mr. A. H. Shultze (1923), was able to identify the most important difference for the racially motivated congress-goer. "Of the head," the exhibitor explained, "the brain part is proportionally smaller . . . in the negro fetuses" than in the white (plate 11). It is interesting, when viewing these models today, to note that regardless of the size of the fetus's brain, comparative measurement of human craniums has often been associated with racist and sexist attitudes.

Consider the case of Samuel George Morton, who, like Shultze, studied comparative brain sizes in terms of race. In the early 1800s Morton assumed that brain size and intelligence were positively correlated and he undertook a study of the cranial capacities of the various human races. When Gould reevaluated Morton's cranial measurement data, he found that despite the fact that "[Morton's findings] matched every good Yankee's prejudice—white on top, Indians, in the middle, and blacks on the bottom," no significant size differences among the craniums of the differing races could be found (Gould, 1981, pp. 53–67). Morton did not lie. He presented all his data; he just misinterpreted them. As Gould points out, Morton's "error" was unintentional. It was based on an unconscious commitment to racial hierarchies. It is this lack of a conspiracy that makes the Morton story of interest. Science, after all, is done by human beings in a social and cultural context and that context can, and often does, have an effect on the work of the researchers. As we will see, it may also have an effect on the work of professional educators.

Did Shultze (1923) also operate with an unconscious belief in the superiority of the Anglo fetuses? We have no way of knowing. He may have had data that supported differing brain sizes. But he did not supply them and we have no way of validating the comparative sizes of the brains themselves. But as the 20th-century philosopher Ludwig Wittgenstein pointed out, context does have a profound effect on meaning (Janik & Toulmin, 1973). And when placed into the context of the Second International Congress of Eugenics, Shultze's studies of comparative brain sizes had a clearly racial meaning. They supported a system of racial hierarchies in which the Anglo-American position was superior to all others.

The proceedings of the 1921 Congress were bound in two volumes, *Eugenics, Genetics, and the Family* (Davenport, 1923a), and *Eugenics in Race and State* (Davenport, 1923b), with many of the papers focusing on the force of heredity and the threat of racial degeneration. One speaker talked of the inevitability of an unequal society and argued that hopes for creating a democratic social order were for naught. "The conclusion appears inescapable," concluded Galton Society member Frederick Adams Woods, "that no matter how much we may contemplate environmental forces making for equality and democracy . . . the real result has been in the opposite direction" (Woods, 1923, p. 321). While some warned of race suicide, others, like the Race Betterment Foundation's Wilhelmine E. Key, observed that "the foundations of national power are in the last analysis biological. Increasingly we are being won over to the view that the elements of a nation's strength lie in the inherent traits and tendencies of its people" (Key, 1923, p. 405). But there were anti-eugenic influences in society and education was to play an important role in their amelioration:

> Among the other means of correcting the anti-eugenic influences now at work to undermine our integrity as a people, we might name the following: A campaign of education among all classes of our population which will foster the eugenic conscience. Many of our people, notably our young women, products of so-called higher education, have been victims of the "ingrowing eugenic conscience" . . . [and] their failure to become parents has meant a distinct national loss. (pp. 410–411)

The point that nature was more important than nurture provoked another speaker to demand a resolution to the debate. "Until we know beyond question," Alleyne Ireland explained,

> whether people are what they are *chiefly* because their forbears were what they were, or are what they are *chiefly* because their contemporaries do to them what they do to them we cannot know whether or not we are trying to force a thousand-dollar education into a one-dollar boy. . . . I commend, therefore, to the serious attention of the Congress the enterprise of appointing a committee charged to investigate and report on the present status of the heredity-environment issue . . . [and] for the dissemination of scientific information on the subject to all educational institutions throughout the world. (1923, p. 426, emphasis in original)

While the record does not indicate whether such a committee was formed, another organization favoring nature over nurture was formed. Three years after assisting in the creation of the Galton Society and planning for the Second International Congress of Eugenics, Madison Grant, Henry Fairfield Osborn, and Charles Benedict Davenport moved to take leadership roles in that new organization—the American Eugenics Society (AES).

During this century's first two decades, American Eugenics narrowed its attention from a general concern for improving livestock to programs of human breeding. As its leadership cadre moved from the American Breeders Association through conferences and congresses on race betterment and eugenics, their attention continued to focus on hereditary control for human improvement. And as we shall see, the movement also continued to express nativist concerns for immigration restriction and ethnic difference. The following chapter continues the analysis of organized Eugenics in the decade after the formation of the American Eugenics Society in 1922. The chapter outlines the activities of the AES as well as those of the Race Betterment Conference in 1928 and the International Congress of Eugenics in 1932.

CHAPTER 2

Organizing American Eugenics: 1922–1932

*The stocks which carry the germ plasm of leadership, talent and ability must be
nurtured and increased, better babies must be the watchword . . . the race must be
purified. Eugenics must be taught throughout our national educational system.*
—L. K. Sadler, A Decade of Progress in Eugenics: Scientific Papers
of the Third International Congress of Eugenics, *1934*

THE AMERICAN EUGENICS SOCIETY (1925)

In the early 1920s the American Eugenics Society (AES) went through a
series of name changes. Initially created as the Ad Interim Committee of
the 1921 Congress of Eugenics, it became the Eugenics Committee of the
United States of America in 1922, the Eugenics Society of the United States
of America in 1923, and finally the American Eugenics Society in 1925
(Laughlin, 1929, p. 4).

As with all well-run organizations, it had an advisory committee
charged to help set policy and organizational direction. It included the
period's leading eugenically committed academics, publicists, politicians,
and psychologists. It is a long list but well worth pondering as its members came from the highest levels of the American academic community
as well as from the fringes of the nativist and racist landscape.

The advisory committee membership included Dr. Carl C. Brigham,
author of *A Study of American Intelligence* (1923); Dr. Henry H. Goddard,
research director of the Vineland Training School and author of *The Kallikak
Family: A Study in the Heredity of Feeble-Mindedness* (1912); Professor Michael
F. Guyer, author of *Being Well-Born: An Introduction to Eugenics* (1916);
C. M. Goethe, director of the Northern California Eugenics League; Professor William K. Gregory, Columbia University professor and secretary
of the Galton Society; Professor David Starr Jordan, president of Leyland
Stanford Junior College; the Hon. Albert Johnson, co-sponsor of the 1924
nativist Johnson-Reed Immigration Restriction Act; Dr. Vernon L. Kellogg,
member of both the National Research Council and the American Breeders Association's Committee on Eugenics; Dr. John C. Merriam, founding
member of the Galton Society and president of the Carnegie Institution in

Washington, DC; Professor Henry Fairfield Osborn, president of the American Museum of Natural History and co-founder of the Galton Society; Paul Popenoe, co-author of *Applied Eugenics* (1918); Lathrop Stoddard, author of *The Rising Tide of Color Against White Supremacy* (1920); Professor Lewis Terman, Stanford University professor of psychology and leader in the American mental testing movement; Professor Edward Lee Thorndike, Teachers College professor of educational psychology and measurement and Galton Society member; and Robert M. Yerkes, president of the American Psychological Association, Harvard professor of psychology, and director of the Army World War I Alpha and Beta Testing Program (Evans, 1931).

With this powerful membership in place, organized Eugenics continued to strengthen its links to American education. By focusing its attention on the schools, the society hoped to promote the incorporation of "eugenics as an integral part of various appropriate courses throughout the school system, in the elementary grades through high school as well as the encouragement of special courses in colleges and universities" (Evans, 1931, p. x). As we shall see in the chapters that follow, the society achieved successes in each and every one of these venues.

In addition to influencing the school curriculum directly, the society wanted to shape popular opinion through the "dissemination of popular education concerning the facts of eugenics by [a variety] of means" (Evans, 1931, p. x), including the general press, lectures, exhibits, books, and pamphlets. Included here were the dual demands of positive and negative eugenics: the encouragement of parentage among those "endowed richly with hereditary traits of demonstrated desirability" and the prevention of the procreation of "those persons socially inadequate because of defective inheritance" (Evans, 1931, p. x).

To these ends, the AES sponsored traveling exhibits at state fairs and exhibitions throughout the 1920s. In 1926, "Mendel's Theatre" was exhibited at the Sesqui-Centennial Exhibition in Philadelphia (Figure 2.1). Exhibits such as these reinforced the idea that complex human traits followed simple Mendelian ratios in a manner similar to the transmission of hair color. In this rigid application of Mendel to humankind, all human traits are presented as expressions of hereditary units that are discrete and that sort themselves in future generations in predictable numerical ratios. Further, these traits are either dominant or recessive. They do not blend. Using this model of "Mendel's Theatre," American Eugenics Society Secretary Leon Whitney explained differences in hair color between parents and their offspring.

The display, "Some People Are Born to Be a Burden on the Rest," used flashing lights to underscore its hereditarian message (Figure 2.2). The exhibit's lights flash in 16-second, 15-second, and 7½-minute intervals. Every

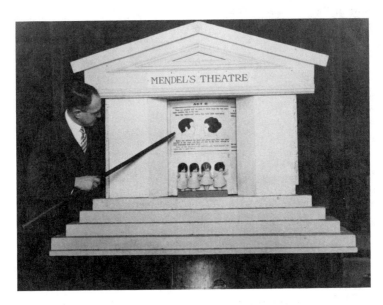

FIGURE 2.1. Dr. Leon F. Whitney using the American Eugenics Society display, "Mendel's Theatre" to lecture on human genetics. Sesqui-Centennial Exhibition, Philadelphia, 1926. Courtesy of the American Philosophical Society, Philadelphia.

16 seconds, the viewer is instructed, a person is born in the United States, and every 15 seconds a person with bad heredity costs the citizenry $100.00. It is only once every 7½ minutes that a person of "high-grade" inheritance is born. To put the message succinctly, a rising tide of bad heredity is threatening the nation's economic well-being. The "burdens" are winning. Lest one miss the implied policy that high-grade individuals marry and have large families, the exhibit also announces an upcoming Fitter Families Contest to be held at the Eastern States Exhibition in Springfield, Massachusetts.

While many today would see such proposals as antediluvian, they were not out of step with their times. They were the proposals of a progressive organization, made during the Progressive Era, and they drew progressive supporters. For example, Margaret Sanger, the champion of birth control, was also a firm supporter of the society's proposals for immigration restriction and marriage laws. Her strongly worded requests for support written to the eugenics popularizer Albert E. Wiggam suggest that she would have supported the society's proposal for the "diffusion of contraceptive information to the 'masses' that they might exercise the control now

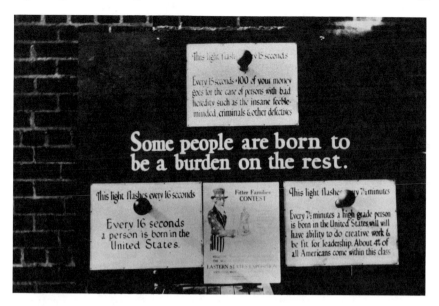

FIGURE 2.2. American Eugenics Society display, "Some People Are Born to Be a Burden on the Rest." Sesqui-Centennial Exhibition, Philadelphia, 1926. Courtesy of the American Philosophical Society, Philadelphia.

exercised by the more favored classes" (Evans, 1931, p. x). It is the blending of eugenical propaganda and class interest that makes these recommendations of interest to us today.

This AES was present as well at the Kansas Free Fair of 1929 where it continued to propagandize the eugenicists' concerns for the production of children of more favored ancestry (Figure 2.3). To counter chance or "blind" sentiment in the production of children, the Topeka fair-goers were instructed that one needs to learn from the mathematical outcomes of fit and unfit crosses in marriage. As the chart makes clear, patterns of "normal," "tainted," and "abnormal" offspring can be seen to follow the ratios that Gregor Mendel described in his research on peas. While T. H. Morgan and his students had shown 14 years earlier that even fruit-fly inheritance was not this simple, the application of Mendelian eugenics to human improvement continued to be promoted by the eugenicists throughout the period.

Progressivism and self-conscious class interest were comfortable bedfellows during this period and the American Eugenics Society was a progressive organization. Our contemporary understanding of the era would be greatly enhanced if we broadened our conception of Progressivism to include modest settlement-house reformers as well as radical biological

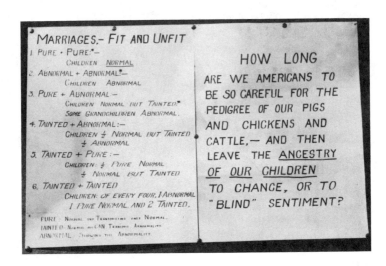

FIGURE 2.3. American Eugenics Society display, "Tainted and Pure Ancestry." Kansas Free Fair, Topeka, 1929. Courtesy of the American Philosophical Society, Philadelphia.

determinists. The continuing belief on the part of many of today's educators that Progressivism was a period of solely liberal motives, actions, and consequences seriously limits our critical abilities. Indeed, many of the insights offered by contemporary historians are based in large measure on the acceptance of the complexity of the period of progressive reform.

Early programs for gifted children exemplify this point. Both conservatives and liberals supported such programs, but for divergent reasons. Conservatives' support for gifted education was consistent with their commitment to a natural *elite*, while liberals did so in terms of their belief in natural *merit*. It would be a mistake not to see both of these positions as progressive; they both believed in a hierarchically ordered society. The issue here is not whether one supports an aristocracy or a meritocracy, but how "natural" either of these socially created categories is thought to be. After all, individuals are situated in either an aristocracy or a meritocracy only after such a social reality is created. We must understand the ways in which such social fictions are constructed if we are to understand how the conservative progressivism of the Eugenics movement legitimated and sustained inequitable social relations in early 20th-century America. It was to such a process of legitimation that the American Eugenics Society turned its considerable energies after 1925.

The society sponsored 16 committees, ranging from Birth Regulation to Social Workers. Understanding the purposes of these committees enables us to see the potential impact eugenics could have on American social and institutional life. For example, the president of the National Committee on Mental Health, an organization identified as a clearinghouse for studies on differential birthrates between superior and inferior stocks, chaired the Committee on Eugenics and Dysgenics of Birth Regulations. With a membership that included University of Wisconsin sociologist Edward A. Ross, the committee recommended differential birthrates for those of greater and lesser worth.

Figure 2.4, also from the Kansas Free Fair of 1929, again uses a series of posters and flashing lights to deliver its hereditarian message. Every 48 seconds, viewers were told, someone was born in America who would never grow up beyond the mental age of 8. In addition, every 11 seconds crime cost America $100,000. And of those who are committed to jail—one every 50 seconds—very few were found to be normal. Once again, crime and poor heredity are linked to create an economic threat. The requirement for programs of negative eugenics seems clear: If the citizenry wants to reduce crime and save the commonweal dollars, a program of sterilization or segregation should be put into action.

One wonders today if recommendations such as these might have been considered by the members of the AES Committee on Cooperation with Clergymen as they read the winning texts from their "sermon contests on eugenics." Quite willing to help the religious in preaching the eugenics creed, that committee supplied "the religious press over the country with eugenical news items and stories as related to religious interest" (Evans, 1931, p. 11).

The society's Committee on Crime Prevention was chaired by Judge Harry Olson. As Chief Justice of the Chicago Municipal Court, Olson had publicly called for the eugenic evaluation of criminals. "If we had a eugenics field worker," he lamented after his indictment of a mass poisoner, "to check up on the history of the whole family at the time one moron was discovered, the police might have been warned to watch this woman" (Haller, 1963, p. 123). While the committee, composed of one judge, one police chief, and six doctors, might have seen the cause of crime as having some environmental dimensions, it is more likely that the chair would have agreed with the Kansas Free Fair exhibit when he reported that "crime is often the result of bad heredity" (Evans, 1931, p. 12).

This issue of the hereditary nature of crime continues to be volatile. When the University of Maryland proposed to hold the National Institute

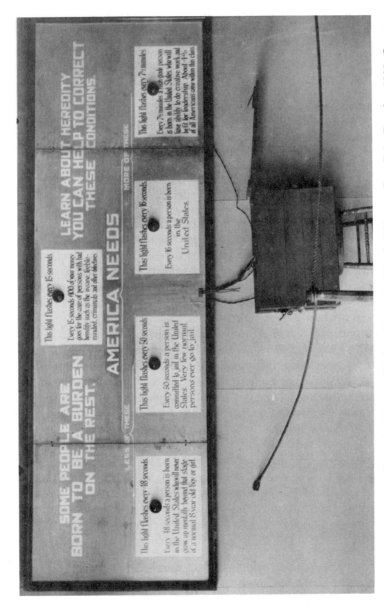

FIGURE 2.4. American Eugenics Society display, "America Needs." Kansas Free Fair, Topeka, 1929. Courtesy of the American Philosophical Society, Philadelphia.

of Health (NIH)-sponsored conference "Genetic Factors in Crime: Findings, Uses & Implications" in the early 1990s, the misplaced public uproar was so strident that the conference funding was withdrawn. By allowing itself to be driven by extreme *anti*hereditarian sentiments, the NIH reversal set a dangerous precedent for academic freedom (Wheeler, 1992, p. A7).

More recently, reports of Dutch research suggesting possible links between genetics and criminal behavior were carried by the national press. Despite the researchers' acknowledgment that their findings were based on a very limited sample of one large family, the public's continuing interest in this topic parallels that of Judge Olson's committee of seven decades ago. In describing this research, the *New York Times* was careful to include Jonathan Beckwith's observation that one of the major limitations of this type of research is that the criminal behaviors have been too poorly defined to clearly identify the dependent variables in those studies. As Beckwith, a molecular biologist at Harvard's Medical School, notes, "it's been a long-term problem in this area. . . . That's one reason why there have been so many announcements of genes that have later been retracted. There's often a lot *less* here than meets the eye" (quoted in Angier, 1993, p. A1, emphasis added).

It was the AES Committee on Formal Education that was charged with promoting the teaching of eugenics in the schools. Sensitive to charges that eugenics was a pseudoscience, it recommended that information on human biology be made by the "method of direct scientific observation rather than by methods of secondhand or hearsay evidence." As the committee's leadership instructed, "by thus substituting direct observation and measurement, both physical and mental, for indirect and uncertain methods, we shall be laying a permanent foundation for the type of research required before eugenics can be accepted on a par with other experimental sciences" (Evans, 1931, pp. 15–16). And when the object of study was mental acuity, the committee recommended the use of the recently developed mental tests. The important role attributed to mental measurements would benefit the eugenicists in at least three ways: First, the use of these tests would aid them in arguing for the hereditary nature of intelligence, a key assumption of the movement. Second, the very fact of administering the examinations would legitimate the tests. And third, it would give professional status to those who administered them.

The use of mental-test data as a basis for social policy was also recommended by the Committee on Selective Immigration. It recommended that restrictions be placed on immigrants "so as to admit only those who are superior to the median American in mental endowment as far as this is shown by approved mental tests" (Evans, 1931, p. 16). As a policy, this superior-to-the-median approach has the disturbing consequence of making the task of gaining entry ever more difficult for each succeeding generation of immigrants. That is, as more immigrants scoring above the median are admitted to these shores, the median score *rises*. This double-edged sword of selective immigration was developed by a committee that included the race thinkers Madison Grant, H. H. Laughlin, and Robert DeCourcy Ward. They penned the committee report and it reflected their extreme nativist biases.

Charter members of the society also included Florence Brown Sherborn, author of *The Child, His Origin, Development and Care* (1934). Her text included both a rendering of Laughlin's Eugenic Tree depicting the centrality of eugenics to all academic "branches" and a photo of the medal presented by the society to the winners of Fitter Families Contests (Sherborn, 1934, p. 11). Whether serving as a committee member, as a professor of child care, or as the chief of the Division of Child Hygiene for the Kansas State Board of Health, Sherborn remained a strong advocate of eugenics. In 1934, for example, she recommended preventing the propagation of the "grossly unfit" through programs of negative eugenics. "No farmer," she explained, "will breed his stock to scrubs, but too often he sanctions the marriage of his children to members of a scrub family" (p. 65). The patrimony in these cases notwithstanding, whether they be persons or cows, Sherborn implied that one way to avoid having one's family turn "scrubby" would be to test potential new members—to have them enter some sort of a competition that evaluated their eugenic fitness.

Such programs were recommended by the Popular Education Committee, which sponsored Fitter Families competitions at fairs in Oklahoma, New York, Kansas (Figure 2.5), Arkansas, Massachusetts, Michigan, Georgia, and Texas during the 1920s. The competitors at these fairs were evaluated by a "staff of authoritative professional people who put . . . families through a searching examination covering heredity, social and educational attainments, and mental and physical status" (Evans, 1931, p. 25). In this way the society could identify the potential parents of a more efficient eugenic future (Figure 2.6). As America and the world teetered on the edge of the century's worst economic contraction, the sponsorship of Fitter Families Contests was transferred to the Race Betterment Foundation. The foundation's 1928 conference proceedings continued to report on those activities (West, 1928).

THE THIRD RACE BETTERMENT CONFERENCE (1928)

The 1928 Race Betterment Conference was again held in Battle Creek and the published proceedings include a completed copy of a Fitter Families Examination Score Sheet. The evaluation records the attributes and achieve-

FIGURE 2.5. Fitter Families Contest Buildings displaying the "Fitter Families for Future Firesides" sign, Kansas State Fair, 1929. Courtesy of American Philosophical Society, Philadelphia.

FIGURE 2.6. Fitter Families Contest Winners, Kansas Free Fair, Topeka, 1923. Courtesy of the American Philosophical Society, Philadelphia.

ments of an anonymous 33-year-old female contestant and it gives today's reader a reasonably clear understanding of the hereditarian biases that shaded the reviewers' judgments.

At the time of her examination, the contestant had graduated from high school, worked as a medical assistant, married, and had brought five of six pregnancies to full term. In addition she had moderate anemia, belonged to the Methodist Church, and had no political affiliations. Recommending that she drink more water and take no coffee, the examining doctors gave her eugenic and individual scores of B plus.

When we consider that this young Michigan woman was in a human capital competition more than six decades ago, her B plus score might lead us to conclude that she must have been an award winner. This was not the case. She was not eligible. Award winners could have no subscore lower than B (West, 1928, p. 98). Alas, this young mother had two B minus scores. Her negatives included "sickness from teeth" and a trace of indol in the urine. Keeping in mind that the eugenic utopia envisioned by the exam's sponsors required that award winners marry award winners, her B minus scores would have serious consequences. Neither she nor her family would be judged worthy of having a place in America's eugenical future and they could never be recipients of the eugenics medal (Figure 2.7) bearing the claim, "Yea, I have a Goodly Heritage" (West, 1928, p. 111).

FIGURE 2.7. Fitter Families Medal Awarded to Prize-Winning Families. Race Betterment Foundation.

What is interesting about the denial of award status for this young mother is that the author of the article recognized that the source of the trace of indol "is likely to be correlated with indifferent health habits" (West, 1928, p. 110). He knew that the cause was environmental. That a 33-year-old housewife with five children would have indifferent health habits certainly seems possible. Indeed it seems probable that she would have had neither the time nor the money to take care of her own health. The point here is that she was not denied access to the winner's circle because of her genes. She was denied access because of her economic status. The eugenic future promised to the winners of the Fitter Families Contests would not only be restricted to the healthy among us. It would also be restricted to the economically well-off.

In 1928, the evaluation procedure for the Fitter Families Contest was that groups of prominent citizens judged participating families for their "ultimate fitness for citizenship and for parenthood" (West, 1928, p. 92). It is obvious that much depended on the ability of the reviewers to render a fair score and participants were reassured that "the contest was fortunate in having excellent individuals for this work" (West, 1928, p. 97). The list included Leon F. Whitney, Dr. Florence B. Sherborn, and Luther West. Whitney was a nonscientist and public relations man who "exhibited such . . . an enthusiasm for extreme eugenics that even Davenport was greatly disturbed" (Haller, 1963, p. 173). Sherborn (Figure 2.8) was associated with the Better Babies Movement from its beginning and would later eschew intermarriage with "scrub" families. Luther West was professor of biology and eugenics at Battle Creek College, and the author of the article in which we read these very reassurances as to the reviewers' competence.

The Fitter Families Contests, which had started in 1914 as the Better Babies Movement, had become, among other things, mirrors of social and class position. For those today who would too quickly rush to judgment, this is not evidence of a conspiracy. The prominent citizen-judges looked at the candidates through their own social lenses; they did not hide traces of indol from the record. Nor did they misrepresent the contestants' physical status. They merely used their own social standards as a basis for their judgments. West (1928) was not unaware of the criticism that the examination forms provided reviewers with scant biological data on the applicants. He admitted:

A very logical criticism of this method of determining an individual's fitness for parenthood may be made on the grounds that it provides no way of arriving at the actual genetic constitution of the individual. We have no method of determining the genetic constitution of plants or animals except by a breeding test, and we may therefore satisfy ourselves with the realization that we are making as close an evaluation of the probable genetic constitution as is humanly possible. (p. 97)

FIGURE 2.8. Mrs. Watts, Florence Sherborn, and Leon Whitney. Kansas State Fair, Topeka, Kansas, 1929. Courtesy of the American Philosophical Society, Philadelphia.

We need to read these assurances carefully today. After all, if the judges lacked objective data in 1928, they would have to use their personal judgments in determining the fitness of the contestants for awards (Figure 2.9). As the reviewers were committed to biological determinism, their use of the contestants' ancestors as proxies for their eugenic worth would certainly seem understandable. Yet this logic ignores the environmental correlates of poor health, of which West was well aware, and it effectively blames the victim for his or her disenfranchisement. In this light, it may not come as a surprise to learn that the examining committee, which included Dr. Luther A. Tarbell among its members, found that "the lad scoring the highest among male children in the Fitter Families Contest" (Figure 2.10) was Luther Tarbell, Jr. (West, 1928, p. 115).

THE THIRD INTERNATIONAL CONGRESS OF EUGENICS (1932)

No Fitter Families Contest reports were associated with the Third International Congress of Eugenics when it held its meeting in New York City in

FIGURE 2.9. Race Betterment Award Given to Individual Prize Winners. Courtesy of the Race Betterment Foundation.

1932. Perhaps that is just as well. After all, the "D" score received by the world's economy in 1932 would probably have reduced the number of contestants who could successfully compete in such contests.

As the Depression deepened, the leaders of American Eugenics joined together for this last formal appeal to the world to save itself by cleaving to the biosociology of hereditarian race betterment. Like a small theater group whose actors had become familiar to the audience even as playbills changed, so the familiar cast presented itself to those assembled at the Museum of Natural History in the late summer of 1932. The program included presentations by Laughlin, Davenport, and Osborn, and reflected their active roles in the movement. The hereditarian extremism that typified their work for almost three decades was still to be found in their conference presentations. In his presidential address, Davenport (1934) looked back on a decade of eugenic progress in sterilization, immigration restriction, and mate selection and noted that in addition to the "marriage advice stations [that] had sprung up in Germany," instruction in eugenics was being offered increasingly in the schools (p. 18).

Underscoring themes he had developed when active in the American Breeders Association three decades earlier, Davenport (1934) called for control of the breeding stock through mate selection, and for increasing

This lad scored highest among male children
entered in the Fitter Families Contest
LUTHER TARBELL, Jr.
Son of Dr. and Mrs. L. A. Tarbell, 21 Green-
wood Ave., Battle Creek

FIGURE 2.10. Luther Tarbell Jr. Fitter Families Contest Winner. Courtesy of the Race
Betterment Foundation.

the number of children from the "more effective, socially more efficient classes." He even went so far as to "rejoice that . . . [the German eugenicist and Hitler's scientific advisor on "Race Hygiene"] Eugen Fisher was entering with enthusiasm into the problem of race crossing over the world" (p. 22). Optimistic about the creation of a superman and a superstate, Davenport identified eugenics as "the most important influence in human advancement." After all, he reminded his audience, "man is an animal, and permanent racial progress in eugenics must be based on the laws of biology" (p. 22). H. F. Osborn (1934), the congress's honorary vice-president, moved in ideological lockstep with Davenport as he explained that environmental reforms were merely "temporary expedients [and that] the only remedy [for society's problems was] birth selection and humane birth control" (p. 29). These extreme Mendelian interpretations placed both men far from the mainstream of biology, and suggestions such as these had virtually no scientific meaning in the context of the genetics of 1932.

As factories closed and millions searched for employment, Osborn (1934) offered hereditarian explanations for economic dislocations. Applying a Spencerian social calculus to these inequities, he found that the Depression had identified the unemployed as candidates for *birth control* while the employed were to benefit from programs of *birth selection*. In what almost seems a parody of science, Osborn presented himself in the role of a disinterested scientist who simply reported that a naturally occurring phenomenon, the economic depression of 1929, had selected the unemployed for extermination and the employed for procreation.

As extreme as these analyses may appear, they were modest by comparison with those of another speaker, who warned that an "aristocracy of the unfit" was rapidly increasing in the United States and that it would "ultimately overrun and destroy . . . the better classes unless a practical program of restrictive eugenics [was] adopted and effectively executed" (Sadler, 1934, p. 193). When the rhetorical question was posed, "Must we sit supinely by and let all this go on?" the answer was immediate and sure, "No! a thousand times, no!" (p. 196).

> The stocks which carry the germ plasm of leadership, talent and ability must be nurtured and increased, better babies must be the watchword . . . the race must be purified. Eugenics must be taught throughout our national educational system. (Sadler, 1934, pp. 198–199)

These demands for racial purity and better babies were already receiving political support in Eugen Fisher's Germany. There, the call to "lay the ax of prevention to the root of the tree of tainted heredity" (Sadler, 1934, p. 200) was becoming policy. While that form of eugenics would never become national policy in the United States, organizations devoted to its dissemination would attempt to influence American schools.

As we shall see, eugenics would never control American education. But its popularization would legitimate hierarchical forms of schooling and programs whose effects were the differential distribution of intellectual capital. Eugenics promoted a concept of schooling as an open market in which individuals competed by means of their inherited traits for high scores—a scarce commodity indeed.

CONCLUSION

In the years between 1903 and 1932, popular eugenics was supported by mainstream members of American society and was embedded in a well-integrated set of national organizations. This chapter has considered nine organizations and conferences in which eugenics held a central place. The list included the American Breeders Association, the Race Betterment Foundation, the Galton Society, the American Eugenics Society, the three Conferences on Race Betterment, and the two Congresses of Eugenics.

Under the active leadership of men such as Charles Benedict Davenport, Harry H. Laughlin, and Henry Fairfield Osborn, among others, these organizations gained the support of many leading American educators for programs designed to use the schoolroom for the popularization and promotion of eugenics. As later chapters will show, Leta Hollingworth, E. L. Thorndike, Robert Yerkes, and W. W. Charters attended these conferences and lent their good names and reputations to the movement. Through their active support they attempted to promote the organizations' policies within the professional educational community.

Despite their use of sophisticated-looking genealogical charts in which they attempted to explain the hereditary nature of human traits, the organization's leaders did not deeply understand the biological mechanisms that they assumed underlay these distributions. By 1932, developments in chromosomal genetics had already surpassed simple Mendelian explanations for human variation. But motivated by racial and ethnic animosities, mainline eugenicists did more than simply organize their like-minded colleagues during this period. They also actively popularized eugenics before the literate public and within numerous professional communities. Let us now turn our attention to the efforts of eugenicists to promote their cause in the classroom itself.

CHAPTER 3

Popularizing Eugenics

When race or national competition becomes sufficiently keen, conscious and well ordered adjustment by eugenic principles will become a powerful educational and sociological weapon which may determine the dominant races of the future. [Today] . . . segregation of classes on ability basis and personal studies are just a few reflections of inheritance differences. Heredity has also to do with vocational guidance. . . . Vocational guidance presupposes a knowledge of inherited abilities, skills likes and dislikes, mental and physical qualities. We are learning to make scientific tests of some of these qualities and here and there we are finding such tests useful in guiding a student to his life work.

—*Dean M. Freeman,*
"Criteria for Judging a Science of Education,"
School and Society, 1929

We have much to learn about eugenics, but even now we know enough to urge us to provide the intellect of man with higher and purer sources than the muddy streams of the past. It is our duty . . . to improve the original inborn ability of man to learn. There is no surer way of improving civilization than by improving man's own nature.

—*Edward Lee Thorndike,* Human Learning, 1931

As we saw in Chapters 1 and 2, the organization of the Eugenics movement in America was driven in great measure by a fear for the allegedly declining quality of the American population. This anxiety also fueled the movement's desire to popularize eugenics in the mind of America's educators. The chapter that follows considers the promotion of eugenics to audiences of educators and the literate public during the first three decades of the 20th century. As we shall see, these efforts focused on the same issues of population control, differential birthrates, selective breeding, and segregation that informed the movement's involvement with other professional groups. It is to a selection of these various venues for dissemination—to newspapers, magazines, popular and educational writings, college textbooks, and teacher training—that we now turn.

E. A. ROSS, "THE INDEPENDENT" (1904)

By 1904 the American Civil War had moved far enough into the historical past for academics of the time to reflect on its impact and its importance. For many this act of reflection was a cause for heightened concern for America's future. Looking back at the 19th century, Stanford sociologist and avid eugenicist E. A. Ross (1904) worried about the war's effects on the American "type." As Ross saw it, "the human stuff here was some carats finer [before the war] than it is today" (p. 1063). The effects of immigration caused Ross additional concern. Sounding a nativist chord not unfamiliar to eugenicists of the period, he argued that while earlier immigration had drawn on Scotch-Irish and Scandinavian sources, the new immigration tapped "lower human levels than the earlier tide" (p. 1063). The current influx was primarily from Croatia, Dalmatia, Sicily, and Armenia, and Ross warned, "they throng to us, these beaten members of beaten breeds" (p. 1063). While America might select from them their best, Ross's biased assessment of their worth seems written between every line of his article from *The Independent*:

> Do these Slovaks and Syrians add as much to the strength of the human piers that support our civilization as the Scotch-Irish or the Scandinavians? As undersized in spirit, no doubt, as they are in body, the later comers lack the ancestral foundations of American character, and even if they catch step with us they and their children will, nevertheless, impede our progress. (p. 1063)

For a progressive nativist such as Ross, who was closely associated with the Social Efficiency Movement in curriculum, race-typing logically informed the negative eugenic policies of immigration restriction and later, "the necessity for sterilization legislation" (quoted in Pickens, 1963, p. 93).

J. F. BOBBITT, "PRACTICAL EUGENICS" (1909)

By 1909, America's anxiety about the effects of the new immigration from Southern and Eastern Europe was crystallized in the popular press by Theodore Roosevelt's term "race suicide." In the period between 1905 and 1909, general magazines published over 35 articles on the topic, which soon became "a minor national phobia" (Higham, 1974, p. 147). In its most benign sense, race suicide simply meant nationalist pride—make America strong. But in its more malignant interpretation, an interpretation popularized by many nativists and eugenicists, race suicide meant racism (Paul, 1995, pp. 100–107). Writing for G. Stanley Hall's *Pedagogical Seminary* in

1909, the educational leader John Franklin Bobbitt (1909) despaired that little could be done for the child of "worm eaten stock." In his article "Practical Eugenics," he called for the careful selection of the parents of the next generation. He argued:

> If the choice could be made with such wisdom and received with such good-will that only children of sound, sane parentage should be born, then our most difficult problems of child training would be solved, most of the evils that pursue humanity would be banished, and the race raised to higher altitudes on its journey toward the Over-man. (p. 385)

While Bobbitt's (1909) excursion to the "Over-man" may have been based on the concept of the Superman from the work of the German philosopher Friedrich Nietzsche, there is little in the article to indicate that he found the trip other than depressing. In the alluvial metaphor often used by eugenicists, he warned that "two sinister processes [were] at work." The first was the "continual drying up of the highest, purest tributaries to the stream of heredity," while the second was "rising flood in the muddy, undesirable streams" (p. 388). For Bobbitt, these sinister forces were unleashed by an irresponsible disregard for the laws of biology. Where "'survival of the fittest' had previously assured that society's best would continue," he warned, "we were now faced with civilization's retrogressive policies. Our schools and our charities," explained this early curriculum reformer, "supply crutches to the weak in mind and morals [and thus] corrupt the streams of heredity which all admit are sufficiently turbid" (p. 387). In this view contemporary civilization served as a buffer between humankind and nature. The negative result was the continuing maintenance of society's least fit. In an earlier period, portrayed by Bobbitt with Nietzsche-like overtones, civilization had not yet thwarted these laws of nature. "In primal days," he explained, "the blood of the race was kept high and pure, like mountain streams." And while

> one may not admire the hard conditions of the savage life of our German forefathers in their Teuton forests; . . . one must admit the high purity of their blood, their high average sanity, soundness and strength. They were a well-born, well-weeded race. (p. 388)

Bobbitt's point was that the processes of nature were not occurring "naturally" enough and that social policy should eliminate artificial barriers in order to permit biological law to work its will. The policy required for this task was, of course, eugenics.

For Bobbitt (1909), eugenics implied a two-part program. First, motivate the strong and capable to increase their number, and second, prevent the "weaklings at the bottom from mingling their weakness in human currents" (p. 392). In discussing possible strategies for the "repression of the unfit," Bobbitt, a founder of the curriculum field, makes a surprising proposal: the "abolition of public charities, public school systems and all other public agencies which go out of their way to preserve the weak and incapable" (p. 393). Bobbitt would later embrace a social efficiency model of educational reform in which a highly efficient citizenry would work toward a corporate rather than a common good. Did this commitment follow from his earlier eugenical insights? After all, if the schools of postwar America could not be eliminated, at least their human charges could be rationally graded and organized in terms of their worth to the state.

Bobbitt probably recognized that the elimination of public schools would be impossible. But the very fact that he made such a recommendation should give one pause. Given his 1909 assumption that schools were too supportive of society's least able, what sense might we make of his prescriptions, nine years later, in his classic education policy text, *The Curriculum* (1918), about the role of the school in society? In that volume, Bobbitt argued that human life was varied and that the central concern of curriculum policy should be matching individuals to the activities of differing social classes. Here we see Bobbitt as a social engineer promoting a blended vision of scientific management, human engineering, and biology, into a theory of curriculum that survives to this day (Kliebard, 1986).

GRANVILLE STANLEY HALL

A third leading American educator whose work and influence are well known to this day was Granville Stanley Hall, who developed Child Study, another major strand of 20th-century curriculum. A prolific writer, Hall authored over 400 articles between 1866 and 1924 and was editor of the *Pedagogical Seminary*, the journal in which Bobbitt's (1909) article appeared.

Hall's pedagogical recommendations sprang from his developmentalist views and from his belief in the determinism of biology. Hall maintained a "preoccupation with what he called 'individualization' [which led] him to prescribe wide variation in what was taught, not only in terms of the great range of intellectual abilities within the school population, but in terms of other genetically determined characteristics such as gender." He further believed that

> nature not only fixed the stages through which all human beings passed, but determined the limits of human educability and, hence, the nature of the social hierarchy. A strong believer in hereditary determinism, Hall advocated

differentiated instruction based on native endowment and even separate schools for "dullards" in the elementary grades. (Kliebard, 1986, p. 47)

Believing in the heritability of the "criminal mind," Hall contended that negative and positive eugenics were necessary components of social policy. As Curti (1935/1959) notes, Hall's views were "on the whole against the prevalent American conception that education is a remedy for social ills."

> Even when [Hall] conceded that eugenics might be a long-run remedy, and that in the meantime education must play a positive role, he still maintained that heredity, and the process of evolution, being what they are, education cannot, even at its best, transform human nature or reverse many of its sets and trends. (p. 413)

While it is inappropriate to draw lines of causality between teacher and student, we do know those Hall directly instructed and we know of the trajectories of their careers. Among his students were J. McKeen Cattell, H. H. Goddard, L. H. Terman, and John Dewey. Certainly he had a differing impact on each of these future educational leaders. All except Dewey were strong advocates of eugenics throughout their careers.

THE EUGENICAL NEWS (1924–1931)

In addition to its dissemination through the professional writings of academics such as Ross, Bobbitt, and Hall, eugenics's putative importance for education was also promoted through newsletters and magazines. One such newsletter, in continuous publication from 1920 to 1938, was the *Eugenical News*. "Avidly racist and restrictionist" (Haller, 1963, p. 149), the *News* was published monthly by the Eugenics Research Association and the Eugenics Society of the United States of America. Associated with the Eugenics Record Office as well, it regularly reprinted the minutes of the Galton Society meetings.

While the influence of the Eugenics movement and race thinking is difficult to trace in many areas, there is no difficulty in identifying one of its greatest political triumphs, the signing of the Johnson Restriction Act on May 26, 1924. *The Eugenical News* found the bill, which limited immigration to a percentage of the national origins of the U.S. population from the 1890 census, "admirable" and indicated that it "demands the support of all eugenists" (*Eugenical News*, 9, 1924, p. 3).

The same issue that lauded the passage of the Johnson-Reed act also contained a review of *White America* by Earnest S. Cox. Supporting the volume's extreme racial antagonisms, the reviewer noted that "the worst thing to happen to the . . . United States was the bringing of large numbers of Negroes, nearly the lowest of races, to our shores" (*Eugenical News, 9,* 1924, p. 3). The reviewer made a biological analogy with his suggestion that it was time for the host to "destroy its parasite." Raising the issue of the presumed corrosive consequences of race mixture for white civilization, the review supported policies of "expatriation [for] Negroes of breeding age to Africa." The editor found "America worth saving for the white race" and opined that Cox "will be a greater savior of his country than George Washington. We wish him, his book, and his 'White American Society' godspeed" (p. 3). For more than a decade the *Eugenical News* championed the notions of the differential worth of races, the idealization of the Nordic, a positive interpretation of authoritarian rather than democratic political orders, and state-sponsored sterilization.

While sterilization laws generally applied only to incarcerated individuals, the *News* (*10,* 1925) was able to report that Oregon had a policy much more to its liking. In Oregon, a "Eugenics Commissioner . . . has the authority to comb the state for degenerates and enforce sterilization" (p. 71). Recalling the earlier accolades heaped on Cox's (1923) racist text, we may well wonder how such proposals for state commissioners might have been taken by the African-American population of the day.

Throughout the 1920s, the *Eugenical News* continued to popularize racist positions at home and totalitarian politics abroad. The February 1928 issue contained two such items. The first detailed the California Immigration Commission's study of the eugenic aspects of immigration. Presenting California as originally "won from Nature by Nordics," the state was depicted as threatened by an "alarming influx of Mexican Peons [who would] inject another serious color problem into American life" (*Eugenical News, 13,* 1928, p. 24) unless they were excluded. The second item summarized a Galton Society meeting during which a representative of Italy's fascist government presented an academic honor to the American Museum of Natural History's president, Henry Fairfield Osborn.

Two years later the *News* would link eugenics and education, citing the New York Commissioner of Education's query that since "the greatest care is exercised in the breeding of live stock, is it not vastly more important that the human race be improved?" and his recommendation that teachers abandon practices that led to the "haphazard mating of human beings" (*Eugenical News, 16,* 1931, p. 6).

While modest in size, the *News* was often quite strident in tone and this might have limited its effectiveness in bringing the credo of eugenics to a broader educational audience. Clearly, a more moderate organ was needed. And so a new journal was created. Published on glossy paper and formally bound, the journal *Eugenics* would give a much more academic veneer to the presentation of the movement.

THE AES JOURNAL, *EUGENICS* (1928–1931)

The Eugenics Record Office (ERO) published the racist tract *Eugenical News* from 1920 to 1938. During the years 1926–1928 and 1931–1938, the *News* was co-sponsored by the American Eugenics Society, which published *Eugenics* from 1928 to 1931. Each issue of *Eugenics* was devoted to a single theme and the title pages featured both Francis Galton's profile and the Fitter Families Contest medal. After *Eugenics* ceased publication, one issue of *People* was published. In 1931, AES again affiliated itself with the *News* and when the ERO was closed in 1938, AES took over the *Eugenical News* as a quarterly, commencing with the March 1939 issue. In 1954 it was replaced with the *Eugenics Quarterly*, which became the *Journal of Social Biology* in 1968.

The lead article of the premier issue of *Eugenics* focused on the links between eugenics and education, which were described by the birth control advocate C. C. Little (1928) as two new and interdependent sciences. Their interdependence was based on education's need for a scientific basis and eugenics's ability to supply it (p. 2). Whether the science is the management theories of Frederick Taylor, the sociology of Talcott Parsons, or the psychology of Burris F. Skinner, the findings of science are regularly offered to educators with a promise of increased professional power and legitimacy. So too it was with eugenics. "Education," Little explained, "has long felt the need for an adequate body of scientific data to provide for it the foundation necessary to any properly established profession" (p. 2). That scientific knowledge was of human mental and physical differences whose transmission followed "definite and highly predictable courses" (p. 2). For the small number of genetic diseases known to be transmitted in Mendelian terms at that time, this observation was justified, but in the case of mental differences, the talk of such "highly predictable courses" was without scientific warrant.

Whether dealing with individuals or with groups, eugenicists always maintained a central interest in population control. Portraying humankind on a normal curve of distribution, they often focused on programs directed at the upper and lower ends of the scale. Not surprisingly, articles supporting both negative and positive eugenics were regularly published in the journal. One such article, by J. H. Kellogg of the Race Betterment Foundation, recommended the creation of a eugenic aristocracy: We need "an aristocracy, a group of men and women who are willing to keep themselves unspotted from the world," he argued, "a nucleus from which in time may develop a new and better human race." In his view, there was little to be gained from environmental reform, "there [was] no hope . . . except for such a plan [of eugenics]" (Kellogg, 1929, p. 16). Those searching for a contemporary example of Kellogg's program need look no further than the California Repository for Germinal Choice, a frozen sperm bank of Nobel Laureate depositors. The genetic inheritance of these men is guaranteed to remain unspotted until a "proper" match is found.

Harsh judgments of society's least able were also made on the pages of *Eugenics*. In terms that sounded much like Bobbitt's, one writer warned that "preserving individuals who would otherwise succumb tends to lower the general standard of efficiency and accomplishment" (Campbell, 1929, p. 3). Another author recommended sterilizing "undesirable types," and charged feminism with the responsibility of saving society. "The feminist movement," this author suggested, "may have arrived just in time to preserve this last civilization from following all its precursors once more into barbarism" (Hodson, 1929, p. 3).

The role of women represented a problem for many eugenicists. In one possible eugenic future, women might be valued in terms of their procreative powers. High-quality women in such a future should be fecund. But some progressive women's groups demanded more than this single definition of womanhood. The problem for *Eugenics*, which advertised itself as "the only journal in the world devoted to a dignified popularization of the subject," was how to respond to these demands. We can find one response in the work of the Norwegian eugenicist Jon Alfred Mjoen (Figure 3.1), who blended the eugenicists' traditional fear of race mixing with a concern for the role of women, and for their education.

While most North Americans would view Norway as a monoracial nation, Mjoen's early work focused on the alleged negative effects of race crossing between Norwegians and Lapps, a minority in that country. A traditional race thinker, Mjoen had made a presentation before the Congress of Eugenics in 1921 in which he supported barriers to interracial unions. He wanted to avoid a "blood mixture between these two races which we will deplore and regret when it is too late" (Mjoen, 1923, p. 60). His presentation exemplified his race thinking, with pedigree charts depicting racial disharmonies, maps and photos showing the characteristics and territories of the Nordic Race, and photos of seminude prostitutes of racially mixed backgrounds. Chase (1977) characterizes Mjoen's presentation as a "perfect burlesque of the Nutty Professor routines so popular in American Vaudeville houses" (p. 284). Mjoen's concluding remarks, however, were considerably less than amusing. *"We shall prevent race crossings not on the ground that we are so much better than all other races,"* he ex-

FIGURE 3.1. Dr. Jon Alfred Mjoen (left), shown here
with Dr. Leon Whitney, Secretary of the AES. Courtesy
of the American Philosophical Society, Philadelphia.

plained. *"We shall love and protect each of us our own race for the same reason
that we love our father and mother: Because it is our race!"* (Mjoen, 1923, p. 61,
emphasis in original). Such racial ideas would play well on the European
continent within the next dozen years.

Writing for *Eugenics* in 1930, Mjoen focused his attention on the education of women. "Young women," he charged, "should learn that where
families are limited to one or two children, the stock in question must inevit-
ably become extinct." Avoiding extinction required, among other things,
a differentiated school curriculum. "Women should not have an inferior
but another education" he explained. They should also have the opportunity for employment, but with one caveat:

> A wise government will in the future work to lead her paths in such direc-
> tions, both for her sake and the welfare of the race and state that she will be
> more and more fit for her divine calling as the renewer, the nourisher and
> the protector of the race. (Mjoen, 1930, p. 326)

Surely such views must be seen as bordering on the totalitarian in both tone
and direction.

Despite Mjoen's limited views on gendered roles, the question of a woman's right to the education and vocation of her choice continued to be debated on the pages of *Eugenics*. When the January 1931 issue featured the symposium "Working Wives and Eugenics," the vote was two to one in favor of women's participation in the work force. Interestingly, the one negative vote was cast by David Snedden, a national leader in the Social Efficiency Movement in education. Snedden (1931) recommended the exclusion of married women from "teaching and other gainful public service employments." He suggested that those concerned with women's education "reexamine their . . . scales of values in light of modern insight and the principles of the greatest good for the greatest number, in the long run" (p. 20). Here again we can see how a concern for social efficiency bound education to eugenics. Snedden, as both educator and eugenicist, advocated the limitation of women's roles in society. For Snedden, social efficiency and gender equality were incompatible. Indeed, for many eugenicists, social equality itself was a problematic policy.

By early 1931, *Eugenics* had ceased publication. Its popularizing responsibilities were transferred to the journal *People*, which published only one issue. By 1939, even the racist *Eugenical News* had changed its tone after its purchase by the American Eugenics Society. Under a new editorial board, the *News* began a campaign of a more moderate nature. This moderation, however, was a change in degree rather than in kind. The commitment was still to the overriding importance of heredity in human affairs and to the valuing of the individual in terms of a corporate reality.

POPULARIZING EUGENICS THROUGH COLLEGE TEXTBOOKS

The period after 1909 also saw an active introduction and expansion of eugenics into the curriculum of numerous top-tier American universities (Selden, 1983). While the study of eugenics entered the curriculum primarily through courses in biology, genetics, sociology, and psychology, many colleges established special courses on the topic. Haller (1963) reports that

> by 1914, Harvard, Columbia, Cornell, Brown, Wisconsin, Northwestern, [and] Clark . . . offered courses devoted in whole or in large part to eugenics. In 1912–1913 Roswell Johnson . . . began a course on eugenics at the University of Pittsburgh . . . [and by that time] a number of texts for college courses appeared. (p. 72)

Eugenics was having an influence on the university course of study as "the number of colleges and universities offering courses in eugenics increased from 44 in 1914 to three hundred and seventy-six in 1928, when according to one estimate, some 20,000 students were enrolled" (Cravens, 1978, p. 53).

When reviewing this period of active popularization, Maurice Bigelow (1946) identified three books that had been well used in the college classrooms of the day. They included Davenport's *Heredity in Relation to Eugenics* (1911), Popenoe and Johnson's *Applied Eugenics* (1918), and Conklin's *Heredity and Environment in the Development of Man* (1923) (p. 49). Let us consider these college textbooks as we examine how they were used to promote and disseminate the creed of eugenics.

HEREDITY IN RELATION TO EUGENICS (1911)

Charles Benedict Davenport was one of the prime movers in the organization of American eugenics, and he was author of the popular college text *Heredity in Relation to Eugenics* (1911). As we learned in Chapter 1, he supported eugenics from his days as director of the Eugenics Record Office in 1904 until his death in 1944. For Davenport, virtually every human trait followed the rules of Mendelian inheritance. It was "not only mental disease and mental deficiency" that were inherited he argued, "but such characteristics as 'shiftlessness,' 'licentiousness,' and 'criminality' [were also] attributed to the presence or absence of one or more Mendelian determiners" (quoted in Rosenberg, 1961/1976, p. 92). Even prostitution was viewed as having a hereditary basis.

As did his eugenical colleagues, Davenport (1911) argued that social improvement could be achieved primarily through hereditarian reform. Changes in the environment, or "euthenical" reform as it was called, were useless. "Modern medicine," he informed his collegiate readers, "is responsible for the loss of appreciation of the power of heredity." In Davenport's view, heredity was the basis for inequality in society; it not only described what individuals could do, but it prescribed what they should do: Medical professionals had forgotten this. They had forgotten "the fundamental fact that all men are *bound* by their protoplasmic makeup and *unequal* in their powers and responsibilities" (p. iv, emphasis in original). Sounding what had become a eugenical commonplace, he informed his readers that "man is an animal and the laws of improvement of corn and race horses hold true for him also. Unless people accept this simple truth," he concluded, "and let it influence marriage selection, human progress will cease" (p. 1).

Combining his Mendelian views with a strong belief in racial differences, he linked skin color to moral and mental qualities. "So far as skin color goes," he explained to his readers, "[mulattos with light skin pigmentation] are truly as white as their greatgrandparent and it is conceivable that they have mental and moral qualities as good and typically Caucasian as he had" (Davenport, 1911, p. 38). There is a compelling variety of racism embedded in this sort of analysis. By viewing social traits in the Mendelian terms of dominance and recessiveness, Davenport could argue for the breeding of particular characteristics regardless of race. "Just as perfect white skin color can be extracted from the hybrid," he explained, "so may other Caucasian mental and physical qualities be extracted and a typical Caucasian arise out of the mixture" (p. 38). Here is the interesting twist: It is not Caucasians per se that are valued more highly than other races; it is rather Caucasian traits that are most advantageous.

For college students using this text in the early years of the 20th century, the message was straightforward enough. Human breeding simply required the extracting of valued traits from the parent hybrid stock. Davenport's *Heredity in Relation to Eugenics* (1911) included lists of legitimate and illegitimate traits taken from the physical, social, and moral realms. The lists included Alkaptonuria, an authentic Mendelizing trait known to be a recessive, as well as shiftlessness, a trait associated with the infamous Jukes family (p. 80), and criminality (p. 85).

Even if Davenport's descriptions of social misbehaviors were accurate, the attribution of hereditary cause is surely open to alternative interpretations. The depictions of the antisocial behavior of families such as the Jukeses may well have been valid, but there is no more reason to believe that they suffered from bad blood than from grinding poverty. One need not excuse criminality in order to reject eugenics. But Davenport supported eugenics and recommended that public school teachers keep careful records of those inferior individuals.

Once again it fell to educators to fulfill this eugenic responsibility. The most likely candidates to undertake such surveys, in Davenport's view, were public school teachers, and he recommended a series of state eugenic surveys to locate "the centers of feeblemindedness and crime and know what each hovel is bringing forth" (Haller, 1963, p. 68). Society, he concluded, "should let the bright light of knowledge into all matters of the reproduction of human traits, as the most dangerous of its enemies or the most valuable of its natural resources" (p. 68).

Here it may be important to reconstruct the relationship between Davenport's eugenic beliefs and his social policy recommendations. Accepting a theory of Mendelian inheritance that viewed hereditary factors as discrete and separable, he viewed individuals as mosaics of traits.

Social improvement was synonymous with increasing desirable and de-creasing undesirable traits in the population. Since individuals were the carriers of these traits, the control of their mating was a central concern of the eugenicists. But notice how Davenport moved from Mendelism to race differences in his evaluation of the effects of immigration on the United States. Waxing historical, he told the story of the State of Virginia, where low-quality stock was replaced by individuals of better heredity. As he explained it, the execution of Charles I caused a large number of royalist immigrants to travel to America's shores. Endowed with supe-rior qualities, these immigrants "enriched a germ plasm which easily developed such traits as good manners, high culture, and the ability to lead in all social affairs—traits combined in remarkable degree in the 'first families of Virginia'" (Davenport, 1911, p. 207). By comparison, the analy-sis of more recent immigrants told a different story. That story permitted Davenport to move easily into ethnic stereotyping. German immigrants, his readers were informed, had a "love of art and music, including the love of song birds" (p. 214), while Italians had a "tendency to crimes of personal violence [counterbalanced by their] capacity for hard monoto-nous labor" (p. 218).

Anti-Semitism and racism were often presented by American nativ-ists as an intellectual pair and such was the case in *Heredity in Relation to Eugenics* (Davenport, 1911), in which undergraduate readers were told of the antisocial traits carried by Eastern European Jewish immigrants. The list included virtually every classical anti-Semitic charge, save for that of Blood Libel. "The Hebrews," Davenport warned, "showed the greatest proportion of crimes against chastity and in connection with prostitution, the lowest of crimes."

> There is no question that, taken as a whole, the hordes of Jews that are com-ing to us . . . with their intense individualism and ideals of gain at the cost of any interest, represent the opposite extreme from the early English and more recent Scandinavian immigration with their ideals of community life in the open country, advancement by the sweat of the brow, and the uprearing of families in the fear of God and the love of country. (Davenport, 1911, p. 216)

Davenport strongly supported policies restricting immigration from South-ern and Eastern Europe. By 1925 he expressed his continuing anti-Semitism when he told a friend:

> Our ancestors drove Baptists from Massachusetts Bay into Rhode Island but we have no place to drive the Jews to. Also they burned witches but it seems to be against the mores to burn any considerable part of our civilization. (quoted in Rosenberg, 1961, p. 96)

The full consequences of these views would not become clear until Germany prepared for the Second World War. At that point restrictions on Jewish immigration would begin to take their toll on the lives of those wanting safe passage out of the maelstrom, and Davenport's wishes would be realized.

STATE LAWS LIMITING MARRIAGE SELECTION IN LIGHT OF EUGENICS (1913)

Ethnic animus was also evident in Davenport's views on interracial marriages in *State Laws Limiting Marriage Selection in Light of Eugenics* published in 1913. Although not on Bigelow's list, it does detail Davenport's extreme views on race. Once again Mendelism was appropriated for racist ends. Among the undesirable unit characteristics of black Americans, Davenport listed

> a strong sex instinct, without corresponding self-control; a lack of appreciation for property distinction (a capacity for which an African origin would hardly have contributed); a certain lack of genuiness—a tendency to pass off clever veneer for the real thing, due to inability or unwillingness to master fundamentals; [and] a premature cessation of intellectual development. (p. 34)

Having diminished Americans of African heritage with the above attacks, Davenport then engaged in a form of paternalism that seems to typify racists in all venues. He reported that full-blooded American Negroes embodied the desirable qualities of "good-nature, keen sense of humor [and] dog-like fidelity . . . when treated kindly" (p. 32). To this list he added keen eyesight, superior hearing acuity, and greater resistance to pain than their white counterparts. Once again this is exemplary of the racist ploy of damning with faint praise. Note that the list focuses on physical but not cognitive or ethical competence. In this rendering, African Americans are depicted as strong but unintelligent, perfect candidates for a paternalistic racism.

Davenport (1913) chided his readers not to think of the characteristics of "black skin pigment, 'wooly' hair, peculiar odor, . . . [and] lack of sex restraint" (p. 34) as necessarily associated; these were separate qualities that could be bred out of the race while the desirable characteristics could be bred in. Recommending that marriage legislation should "forget skin color and concentrate upon matters of real importance to organized society," he demanded that those without sex control or educability be prevented from reproducing. His recommended methods included "segregation during the reproductive period, or even, as a last resort, sterilization" (p. 36). Yet race is never far below the surface as he prescribed that,

> No person having one-half part or more Negro blood shall be permitted to take a white person as a spouse [and] any person having less than one-half, but not less than one-eighth part of Negro blood, shall not be given a license to marry a white person without a certificate from the State Eugenics Board. (p. 36)

This modification of the marriage selection laws would codify the existing laws restricting marriage at a higher level of bureaucratic sophistication. In Maryland, for example, a 1913 law labeled racial intermarriage of white and Negro or descendant of a Negro to the third generation as an "infamous crime" to be "forever prohibited and void." In addition, the law required a maximum penalty of 10 years imprisonment plus a $100 fine to the minister performing the union. The Davenport modification added to these caveats an evaluation by a State Eugenics Board—a board likely to be in sympathy with the view of such marriages as infamous crimes. It was, in fact, not until 1967, with *Loving versus Virginia*, that laws restricting racial intermarriage were judged unconstitutional by the U.S. Supreme Court.

We must, Davenport (1913) concluded, "increase the density of socially desirable traits in the next generation—by education, segregation and sterilization; and by keeping out immigrants who belong to defective strains" (p. 36). In this last caveat we see that the alleged "separate" characteristics of immigrants, at least, have been replaced by interpretations that can only be seen as racist.

Reading these noxious comments in today's context may well give the reader pause. One may legitimately wonder what benefit is gained from the repetition of this racist and anti-Semitic commentary. The answer comes later in this chapter, when we consider Davenport's association with teacher education programs in the 1920s. We shall see in the next chapter that his work was regularly cited in high school science textbooks published between the wars. Yet his influence on American education is little known today. We need to understand his racial positions, destructive as they were, if we are to ask substantive questions about his association with many seemingly progressive educational policies and programs.

The point here is that proposals for negative eugenics were not foreign to the United States. Nor were they an unknown in the American school curriculum. Writing from his vantage point in 1946, Bigelow recalled that "between 1910 and 1920 there was much interest in eugenics as a topic in biology courses in senior high schools and colleges," and heading the list of the volumes "most commonly cited for reference" was *Heredity in Relation to Eugenics* (p. 49).

APPLIED EUGENICS (1918)

When Paul Popenoe and Roswell Johnson published their college textbook, *Applied Eugenics*, in 1918, they cited Davenport's work for reference and support. *Applied Eugenics* was to be a volume that would emphasize "the practical means by which society may encourage the reproduction of superior persons and discourage that of inferiors" (p. v). They were also quite clear that education, particularly compulsory education, had a significant role to play in achieving those goals. "The educational system," they explained, "should be a sieve through which all children in the country are passed . . . which will enable the teacher to determine just how far it is profitable to educate each child that he may lead a life of greatest possible usefulness to the state and happiness to himself" (p. 370).

At a certain level this seems a reasonable, if not in fact a progressive, suggestion. After all, shouldn't community members maximize both the community's and their own possibilities? A more careful reading of the text suggests that the authors' purpose had less to do with maximizing individual potential than with classifying individuals into existing social categories. "It is very desirable," Popenoe and Johnson (1918) instructed their undergraduate readers, "that no child escape inspection, because of the importance of discovering every individual of exceptional ability and inability" (p. 371).

Such identifications were needed not simply for the happiness of the individuals in question, but for an efficiently run state apparatus in which schools, military, and procreative control could be linked. National evaluation programs of this sort would probably become a function of the school, they explained, "owing to the great public demonstration of psychometry now being conducted at the cantonments for the mental classification of recruits" (Popenoe & Johnson, 1918, p. 371). Cutting through the rhetorical style of the early 20th century, we find that Popenoe and Johnson were talking about the racially informed Army Alpha and Beta intelligence test programs. Linking eugenics, schooling, and population control, Popenoe and Johnson concluded that "compulsory education, as such, is not only of service to eugenics through the selection it makes possible, but [it] may serve in a more unsuspected way by cutting down the birth-rate of inferior families" (p. 371).

Having integrated education and negative eugenics, the authors went on to warn their readers against supporting old age pensions and trade unions, as these dysfunctional social policies would decrease the quality of the population. The logic of the argument is fascinating to follow. Popenoe and Johnson (1918) explained that without benefit of pensions, the inferior old would have to live with and be supported by their inferior children. Given the economic demands of this support, they would probably produce fewer inferior children of their own.

Labor unions, on the other hand, were dysgenic because of their demands for regulated hourly wages. Since Popenoe and Johnson (1918) "understood" that all were not equal, it made no eugenic sense to pay all laborers of a given classification the same salary. Indeed, workers of better heritage should be paid in order that they might support larger families. In Popenoe and Johnson's world of labor, capital could organize while workers would remain independent actors. That such an approach would empower the interests of capital over labor was merely an unanticipated consequence of their eugenic policies.

It was in Popenoe and Johnson's (1918) discussion of war that the categories of social efficiency, eugenics, and racism come most clearly and disturbingly into focus. By 1918, their interpretation of the consequences of war takes an ugly turn as they conclude that

> in the United States are millions of negroes who are of less value than white men in organized industry but almost as valuable as the white, when properly led, at the front. It would appear to be sound statesmanship to enlist as many negroes as possible in the active forces, in the case of war, thus releasing a corresponding number of more skilled white workers for the industrial machine in whose efficiency success in modern warfare largely rests. (p. 319)

By 1935 *Applied Eugenics* was in its third edition and these extreme policy recommendations no longer appeared in the text. Yet the authors still argued for a eugenic analysis of American national progress, for race differences, for the "maintenance of the color line," and for an education for African Americans "guided by the results of psychological tests showing the nature of Negro mentality and emotional make-up" (1935, pp. 302–305). Recommendations for programs of negative and positive eugenics were still included, but now it was suggested that each race adopt these practices independently. While Popenoe and Johnson no longer advocated the notion of the differential use of the citizenry as cannon fodder in 1935, their more moderate approach still kept African Americans separate and unequal. Such observations would surely be consistent with the segregated realities of most Ivy League readers during that time.

In keeping with this moderation, Madison Grant's *The Passing of the Great Race* (1921) was eliminated from the 1935 reprint. Grant's work had been present in many college classrooms of the period.

THE PASSING OF THE GREAT RACE (1921)

As president of the American Zoological Society, trustee of the American Museum of Natural History, and co-founder of the Galton Society, Grant was a man of significant social and political influence. He was also one of the nation's foremost racists. He was the author of *The Passing of the Great Race* (1921), a book that became a best-seller. It was yet another volume that popularized eugenics in the college classroom of the 1920s. Basing its policies on a less than genteel racial interpretation of the Army intelligence tests, its primary lesson was that the white race, and particularly the Nordics, were threatened by the internal danger of race suicide. It "is from within and not from without [that the white race is threatened]," Grant explained.

> Neither the black, nor the brown, nor the yellow, nor the red will conquer the white in battle. But if the valuable elements in the Nordic race mix with inferior strains or die out through race suicide, then the citadel of civilization will fall for mere lack of defenders. (p. xxxi)

But external forces were thwarting the successful propagation of his message. Revealing a taste for a totalitarian social order, he complained that "it is the unquestionable fact that there is less freedom of press [in a democracy] than under autocratic forms of government." To this claim he added conspiracies of an international type. It was difficult to transmit his racial truths internationally, he explained, because in France "Jewish influence [is aimed at] suppressing any suggestion of racial differentiation" (Grant, 1921, p. xxxii).

The Passing of the Great Race is a classic example of the racist tract. As with the work of many mainline eugenicists, the volume was filled with racial and gender stereotyping. In its pages, women exhibited the "older more generalized and primitive traits of the race" (Grant, 1921, p. 37); Spaniards were "superstitious and unintelligent" (p. 53); the Irish and Serbs were obsessed with "delusions of former greatness" (p. 53); Americans of African descent became "willing followers who ask only to obey and to further the ideals and wishes of the master race" (p. 87). The significance of the term "master race" should not be lost on today's readers. Many of Grant's views and prescriptions were present in the racial policies of the National Socialist government in Germany in the 1930s. Indeed, the text proposes the elimination of social failures through segregation and sterilization as "a practical, merciful and inevitable solution." Grant further recommended that these policies can be applied to an ever widening circle of social discards, beginning always with the criminal, the diseased and the insane and extending gradually to types which may be called weaklings rather than defectives and perhaps ultimately to worthless race types. (p. 51)

Once again, it is important to recognize that Grant's (1921) policies for the elimination of races were not the rantings of an individual at society's fringes. Nor was his work ignored by educated members of the community. He was a member of New York's social aristocracy, and *The Passing of the Great Race* was a popular text read at the very highest levels of American society. The dust jacket of the 1921 edition quotes a review from the *Saturday Evening Post*, recommending this as one of the "books every American should read if he wished to understand the full gravity of our present immigration problem." On the book's dust jacket, the reviewer applauded it as a "capital book; in purpose, in vision, in grasp of the facts" and showing a "fine fearlessness in assailing the popular and mischievous sentimentalities . . . and corroding falsehoods which few men dare assail," and charged that "Americans should be sincerely grateful to [Grant] for writing it." The reviewer giving thanks in this case was Theodore Roosevelt.

This was a volume whose popularity should not be underestimated. By 1921 it was in its fourth edition, having gone through six printings. During this same period, when Grant and Roosevelt were touting the benefits of eugenics to the general public, similar efforts were under way at meetings of America's premier educational leadership organization, the National Education Association.

BIOLOGICAL DETERMINISM AND THE NEA (1916–1922)

Presentations at the annual meetings of the National Education Association (NEA) often reflected the popular topics of the day and this was certainly true in the case of Dr. Helen Putnam's report at the 1916 conference. That presentation, "The New Ideal in Education—Better Parents of Better Children," continued the popularization of eugenics before an assembly of American educators. "If humanity is to survive," Putnam informed her audience of teachers and administrators, "individualism and nationalism must conform to the laws of racial well-being" (Putnam, 1916, p. 242). While it would have been possible for Putnam to draw on the work of the environmental critic Jacob Riis for such laws, this was not her choice. The laws that Putnam identified were the laws of Mendelian eugenics.

It is interesting to see how Putnam's (1916) interpretations of these laws led her to view citizens as social means rather than as social ends. When discussing the quality of the "millions of Indians and half-castes" in South America, for example, she pointed out that "some of them in all probability [have] qualities desirable to conserve in the racial inheritance" (p. 242). This initially sounds like a humane concern for the dispossessed. But it is a concern rationalized by reference to the contributions that the downtrodden might make in perfecting the race. The individuals themselves appear to have little intrinsic worth except as carriers of those qualities.

We see a similar line of reasoning in Putnam's (1916) concern for the millions of children under 5 years old who died annually in the United States. "Not all the children who die are inferior," she explained, adding that "we have no reason for thinking that even the majority are" (p. 244). Once again Putnam's mourning was not so much for the loss of the lives of these children as it was for the loss to the race that the superior among them represented. It is true that Putnam found North American children and the South American poor worthy of being saved. But they were to be saved primarily for the race's biological well-being, not for their own inherent worth. For those who would distinguish between instrumental valuing that views citizens primarily in their corporate context and more intrinsic democratic values that value the individual as an individual, Putnam's ethical calculus should be a source of concern. It should be noted that the instrumental valuing of human beings has historically been integral to totalitarian, not democratic, states.

Putnam (1916) applied this same rationale of valuing the collective over the individual when describing the plight of working people. Here her concerns were for their free time and marriage choices; in her view, even a 60-hour work week left people with too much free time. It was in these "unoccupied intervals," she warned her listeners,

> that most of the crimes against that race are committed. Spending wisely is harder than earning [and] society does not profit when its educational product earns twenty-five dollars a week and for example, chooses a mate whose father was a moron. (p. 244)

Aided by an anonymous $4,000 donation, Putnam expanded the NEA's popularization of eugenics to include programs of teacher education. Moving to involve institutions of higher education, she "invited certain institutions training educators—universities, colleges and normal schools . . . to cooperate in studying the proposition that 'The supreme object of education should be to make the next generation better than living generations'" (p. 252). Facilitating this goal were $250 honoraria for college graduates undertaking studies of "special excellence" and "about one thousand men and women training to become educators [were] definitely engaged in this study" (p. 252).

Since these were competitive awards, an advisory committee to judge the proposals was formed. And here we return to an individual who has taken much of our attention in the proceeding chapter. Among those listed as the committee specialist was Charles Benedict Davenport (Putnam, 1916, p. 252). Such was the remarkable breadth of the man's organizational involvement. This was, of course, the very same Davenport who had lamented his inability to burn Jews; who had identified the peculiar racial traits of African Americans; and who had found prostitution a hereditary condition. Links between Davenport and the NEA most certainly do not make the NEA a racist organization, nor do they make teachers advocates of his racist and anti-Semitic antagonisms. But they do show how effective American eugenics was in bringing its most extreme views to the attention of American educators.

In the 5 years following its 1916 report, Putnam continued to be active, and in 1921 she addressed the NEA as chair of the Committee on Racial Well-Being. This time college seniors preparing for careers in teaching received a sharper challenge: "It is as much the duty of educators to assure through educational procedures that individuals shall be well born as that they shall be well reared" (Putnam, 1921, p. 362). Ever committed to practical classroom activities, the committee called for exemplary methods to develop "racial ideals" across all grades that would "secure lessened rates of life blunders and life failures" (p. 362). Once again, prospective teachers were warned not to ignore the overriding importance of heredity in life decisions and to take heed of the teachings of eugenics.

In 1922, the committee reported awarding two honoraria—the first to a civics class at the Wisconsin State Normal School in Milwaukee, the second to students studying psychology at the University of Wyoming. Honorable mentions went to the Massachusetts Agricultural College at Amherst and to the La Crosse State Normal School. In addition, the committee reported that Dr. Putnam would be present as an invited delegate at the Second International Congress of Eugenics to be held later that year.

The report ended with a reprint of the April 1917 *NEA Bulletin* call for eugenically oriented studies (*NEA Bulletin*, 1917, pp. 36–38). "It is desired," the awards announcement explained, "that all classes understand the elementary form of Mendel's theory of inheritance of unit characters . . . as they effect [*sic*] human beings" (Putnam, 1922, p. 563). These were the very principles, in their most extreme interpretations, on which Grant and Davenport had built their careers. They were the principles that Putnam had propagated. Oversimplified and bereft of scientific warrants as early as 1915, these Mendelian eugenic principles were still being used by members of the National Education Association in shaping programs for the normal school training of teachers in the 1920s. In some ways Helen

Putnam's most egregious error was taking a rather naive view of our democratic social order and significantly misunderstanding the genetics of her day.

HEREDITY AND ENVIRONMENT
IN THE DEVELOPMENT OF MAN (1923)

When Princeton's Edwin G. Conklin published the third edition of *Heredity and Environment in the Development of Man* (1923) one year after Putnam's last report, he at least was aware that genetics had gone through monumental change. He recognized that analyses of human inheritance had moved from Mendelian factors to a focus on genes and chromosomes. As with other geneticists in 1923, he understood that the heritable material took the form of genes located on string-like chromosomes, rather than discrete, independent factors.

At this point in the development of genetics it was also understood that chromosomes might "cross over" each other during cell division. Such crossing over could lead to the exchange of genetic material and introduce a level of contingency into human inheritance that Mendelian eugenicists had never contemplated in their simple mathematical models. In addition, the chromosomal theory held that genes were linked together and that environment could play an important role in an organism's development. As a consequence of the discoveries that were made in genetics between 1910 and the 1930s, the Mendelian eugenicists' plan to remove a single character and its trait from a human population through simple programs of controlled breeding was recognized as a virtual impossibility. The genetic possibilities raised by crossing over and the linkage of genes on chromosomes made programs based on single factor–single trait eugenics problematic, to say the least. Evidence of Conklin's understanding of these changes is reflected in the inclusion of a gene map of the fruit fly, *Drosophila*, and a discussion of human chromosome numbers in *Heredity and Environment in the Development of Man* (Conklin, 1923, pp. 162–163).

If these transformations in genetics made human single character–single trait arguments questionable, they still left the nature–nurture argument alive and well. In that debate Conklin (1923), still a strong supporter of eugenics, was easily able to choose sides. "So far as organisms below man are concerned," he explained to the collegiate readers of this popular text, "there is general agreement that heredity is the most important factor, and this opinion is also held for man by those who have made a thorough study of heredity" (p. 253). The single example he supplied of such a student of nature was Sir Francis Galton. That Galton had judged nature of greatest import in human development should have come as no surprise to Conklin's readers. After all, it was Galton who founded eugenics.

Conklin (1923) was aware of the power of environment in human development. But he found environment little able to improve humankind. In his view, environmental pressures only highlighted human frailties. If the "prevalence of crime, alcoholism, depravity and insanity . . . [is] a protest and menace of weak men against high civilization," he explained, then the answer is to manipulate the heredity of the population. "We are approaching the time," he informed his readers, "when one or the other must give way, either the responsibilities of life must be reduced and the march of civilization stayed, or a better race of men, with greater hereditary abilities, must be bred" (p. 256). Having thus resolved the nature–nurture debate in favor of nature, Conklin moved to a discussion of the ethics. Should human evolution be controlled? Indeed it should, he answered; through programs of negative and positive eugenics, "the worst types of mankind may be prevented from propagating and the best types may be encouraged to increase and multiply" (p. 292). The aim was to develop what he identified as the "generalized type," which would "include the best qualities of many types and many races" (p. 342).

These qualities would soon become better classes. The transformation can be seen in Conklin's (1923) nativist concern for the declining birthrates of groups he judged most worthy. "The descendants of the Puritans and the Cavaliers," he despaired, "who have raised the cry for fewer and better children are already disappearing . . . [while] in Massachusetts the birthrate of the foreign born is twice that of the native population" (p. 311). His recommendation for increasing families of the better types was matched with the political vision that individuals were to be "subordinated to racial welfare" (p. 311). It was a vision of a corporate order, actually a biological corporate order, in which an individual's importance would be rationalized into the "great organism of humanity" (p. 342). There is an interesting parallel here between the plea for corporate form in biological improvement and the similar corporate claims being made in business, industry, and the schools of the period.

CONCLUSION

It is not necessary to search for conspiracies in order to recognize that individuals and groups interested in promoting their hereditarian ideals in the public policy arena would advocate these views wherever possible. This chapter has highlighted the ways in which the popularization of eugenics paralleled its organization during the first three decades of this century,

and has traced its propagation through analyses of selected journals, magazines, college textbooks, and teacher training programs from 1904 through
the early 1930s. If organizing and popularizing were necessarily the movement's first two steps, then influencing curriculum content would be a
logical third. We turn now to the impact of eugenics on the school curriculum in the period 1914 to 1948.

CHAPTER 4

Eugenics and the Textbook

Hundreds of families such as [the Jukes and the Kallikaks] . . . exist today, spreading disease, immorality, and crime to all parts of this country. . . . They not only do harm to others by corrupting, stealing, or spreading disease, but they are actually protected and cared for by the state out of public money. Largely for them the poorhouse and the asylum exist. They take from society but they give nothing in return. They are true parasites.
—*George William Hunter,*
A Civic Biology Presented in Problems, *1914*

There is no real evidence that the environment changes the intelligence of people. Those of low-grade intelligence would do little better under the most favorable conditions possible, while those of superior intelligence will make good no matter what handicaps they are given.
—*George William Hunter,* Life Science: A Social Biology, *1941*

American eugenicists regularly recommended using the schools as a pulpit for their message of hereditarian reform. An analysis of textbook content (the commodified curriculum) will give some indication of their success in this effort. Of the numerous high school biology texts published in the United States between 1914 and 1948, 41 have found their way onto the shelves of the National Institute of Education Library's archive in Washington, D.C.

The analysis of these textbooks will be presented in two sections. The first offers a statistical rendering of the presence of eugenics in the textbooks. The second focuses on a close reading and unpacking of the text's eugenically oriented policy recommendations. This dual approach will allow the reader to gain insight into both the content and the texture of the arguments offered by these textbooks in their support of eugenics during the 34-year period between 1914 and 1948.

QUANTITATIVE ANALYSIS OF THE BIOLOGY
TEXTBOOKS: 1914–1948

This chapter begins by asking eight questions regarding the presence of eugenics as a topic in those 41 textbooks. The findings here are quite striking. To questions regarding the presence of eugenics in the textbooks, the answers are overwhelmingly in the affirmative (Figure 4.1). Over 87% of the volumes included eugenics as a topic and more than 70% recommended eugenics as a legitimate science.

Eugenics was certainly present in the textbooks. But what was the nature of the evidence marshaled in its support? A third question focuses on the rationale the books offered for the transmission of complex human characteristics. Evidence that identified the specific role that genes and chromosomes might have played would be the most useful in supporting the eugenicists' policies. This is not the level of evidence that these texts presented, however. (Figure 4.2).

Almost 27% reported the that traits "ran" in families, while 22% reported that "blood tells." These are hardly scientific data sets. While genetic interpretations of development using chromosomes and genes were

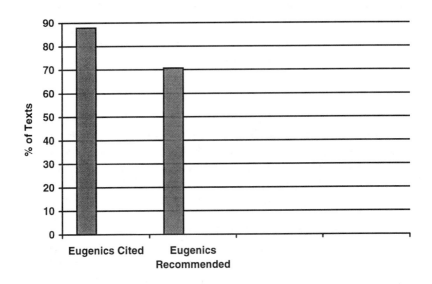

FIGURE 4.1. Presence of Eugenics in High School Biology Textbooks, 1914–1948.

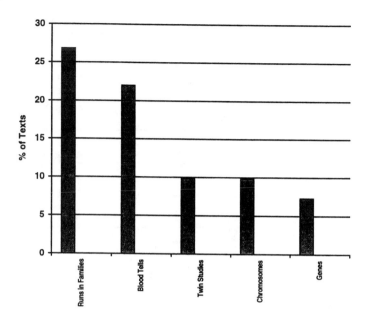

FIGURE 4.2. Eugenic Evidence Cited By High School Biology Textbooks, 1914–1948.

available to the authors for use in their arguments, they appear in less than 10% of the books under consideration.

In the 1920s and 1930s, anxiety about a rising tide of feeblemindedness was fueled in no small measure by H. H. Goddard's famous volume, *The Kallikak Family: A Study in the Heredity of Feeble-Mindedness* (1912). A fourth question asks about the presence of such allegedly inferior families in the textbooks (Figure 4.3).

The Kallikak family, leading a list of other "inferior" lines, was cited in over 60% of the volumes. Also included were the equally infamous Jukes family and the family line of the less well-known Ishmaelites. Data such as these would probably be used to support recommendations for negative eugenics.

As we saw in Chapter 2, the American Eugenics Society regularly held Fitter Families Contests at state fairs during the 1920s. A fifth question asks whether fitter family lines found their way onto the pages of the biology texts under consideration (Figure 4.4).

The answer again, is yes. Most frequently cited were the Edwards, an old Anglo-saxon line, which received the attention of 54.7% of the books. The volumes also included the Bachs (14.6%), the Darwins (9.8%), and the

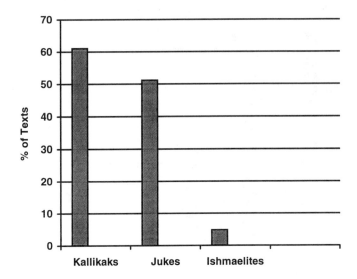

FIGURE 4.3. Inferior Families Cited in High School Biology Textbooks, 1914–1948.

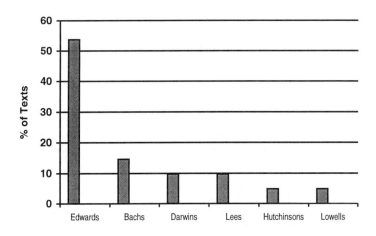

FIGURE 4.4. Superior Families Cited in High School Biology Textbooks, 1914–1948.

Lees (9.8%). The supposed excellence of these families is not at issue here; it is the explanation for their performance that is the question. For the biology textbooks in this review, the answer was an easy one to construct: It was their superior heredity that made these families superior.

A sixth question concerned the hereditary traits that the textbooks presented to their high school readers (Figure 4.5).

It is not surprising that schoolbooks would most frequently list intelligence as inherited. 36.6% of the books cited intelligence as an inherited trait. This was followed by a mix of traits including eye color (14.6%) as well as thrift (7.3%) and morality (7.3%).

Chapters 1 and 2 introduced some of the men and women who were actively involved in the Eugenics movement early in this century. A seventh question searched for the names of those activists as they might have appeared in the textbooks (Figure 4.6).

Many familiar names appear in a significant percentage of the texts. They include Davenport (34.1%), Galton (26.8%), Goddard (24.4%), Wiggam (17.1%), and Popenoe and Johnson (12.2%). While the issues of race and ethnicity are never explicitly discussed, it is interesting to note that it was

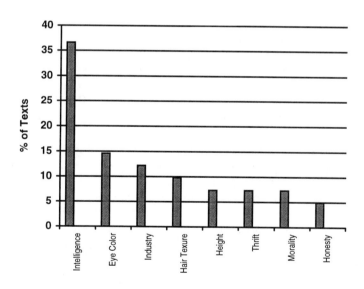

FIGURE 4.5. Inherited Qualities Cited in High School Biology Textbooks, 1914–1948.

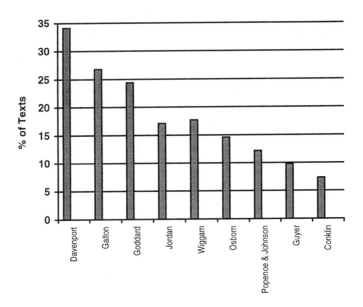

FIGURE 4.6. Eugenic Leaders Cited in High School Biology Textbooks, 1914–1948.

Charles Davenport who wanted to burn Jews; Paul Popenoe who wanted to send African Americans to war to die while saving their Anglo counterparts; H. H. Goddard who wanted to sterilize all high-grade morons; and Alfred Wiggam who thought Jesus was a eugenicist. Perhaps the texts did not have to present racist or nativist notions explicitly. Privileging authors such as these may have been quite sufficient to transmit their messages as a subtext.

Since these activists lobbied for programs of immigration restriction, sexual segregation, and population control, the eighth and last question asks whether any of those policies found their way into the textbooks under review. Again the answers are in the affirmative (Figure 4.7).

The textbook data are striking in this regard as well. Programs of selective breeding were most frequently recommended to the high school reader: Positive eugenics, which called for the selective matings of those judged as society's best, was cited in 64.4% of the texts, and negative eugenics, which demanded the restriction of child-bearing by those judged socially inferior, appeared in 46.3% of the volumes. In addition, 19.5% of the texts recommended immigration restriction and 14.6% suggested policies of segregation and sterilization.

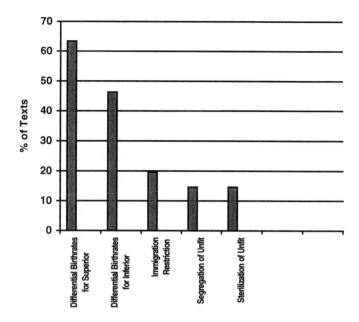

FIGURE 4.7. Social Policies Recommended by High School Biology Textbooks, 1914–1948.

It is clear from these data that eugenics significantly penetrated the high school biology curriculum between 1914 and 1948. While these findings should not be completely unexpected, it is surprising that the training of today's professional educators includes so little evidence of eugenics' impact on the curriculum. After all, that impact included not merely the introduction of a particular content to the texts, but the inclusion of a particular social vision as well—a social vision in which persons were to be judged on their inherited biological merit and then rationally assigned a place in a static and unequal social order.

It is important to repeat that none of the texts reflected overt racial bias. The arguments were never made in terms of race. They were made only in terms of biological merit. Support for this reform or merit-based eugenics is not without its serious limitations, however. As Kevles notes, "reform eugenics was in part self-deluding; notions like 'anti-social character' and 'levels of highest activity' were freighted with class-dependent biases" (Kevles, 1985, p. 176).

We should find these observations neither surprising nor depressing. In a hierarchical social order it is quite possible that the texts' authors were simply reflecting their social class location and their political common sense.

If today's social vision and common sense have changed, so much the better. But ignorance of that past is still unwise.

The point here is not to disregard the findings of genetics. Biological knowledge makes demands on us and it does inform social policy. It would be both foolish and irresponsible to argue otherwise. If the scientific facts are warranted, they demand our attention. Contemporary examples of such data include our increased understanding of the genetic basis for particular single-gene defects such as Tay-Sachs and Huntington's Disease. The knowledge that one is a carrier of such genetic vectors suggests potential avenues for individual choice, rather than state intervention and social "engineering." However, when most of these textbooks were published, information on the basis for numerous genetic conditions was simply unavailable, to say nothing of evidence for the heritability of intelligence or thrift.

At this point we move from a statistical analysis of the texts' contents and policies to a close reading of the texts themselves. It is important, in a metaphorical sense, to let the volumes speak, to let them articulate their vision of eugenics' place in the curriculum and in the broader social order. To that end I have selected biology texts by six authors for close analysis and consideration.

QUALITATIVE ANALYSIS OF THE BIOLOGY
TEXTBOOKS: 1914–1948

The first of the textbooks we consider was written by George William Hunter and published by the American Book Company in 1914. In the years between 1914 and 1941 American Book would publish nine volumes by Hunter. Enough is known about the financial requirements of the publishing industry to conclude that American Book's continuing publication of Hunter's work reflected an acceptable return on the publisher's investment (Apple, 1986). This lengthy publication record is also strong evidence that the books were well received by the school community of the day. Hunter's texts have also been included because they exemplify an author and a publisher who maintained a 27-year commitment to eugenics as legitimate science despite transformations in the parent discipline of genetics itself. Six of the volumes in the following review were authored by Hunter.

A Civic Biology: Presented in Problems (1914)

The first of Hunter's texts is *A Civic Biology: Presented in Problems*, published in 1914. This is the first of the biology textbooks in this review to define eugenics. Noting that human betterment requires personal hygiene, an improved environment, and the selection of healthy mates, Hunter concludes that eugenics means "freedom from certain germ diseases which might be handed down to [one's] offspring." The list includes tuberculosis, epilepsy, feeblemindedness, and a compendium of afflictions that were "not only unfair, but criminal to hand down to posterity" (Hunter, 1914, p. 261). While not presented as the singular cause for differences in human development in 1914, heredity is still seen as a major factor in human improvement.

Citing the studies of the Jukeses and the Kallikaks, Hunter warns his readers that

> hundreds of families such as . . . [these] exist today, spreading disease, immorality, and crime to all parts of this country [where] they not only do harm to others by corrupting, stealing, or spreading disease, but they are actually protected and cared for by the state out of public money. Largely for them, the poorhouse and the asylum exist. They take from society but they give nothing in return. They are true parasites. (Hunter, 1914, p. 263)

Reflecting a theme common to many of these high school texts, negative social traits are seen as running in families and generally impervious to environmental influence. Typical as well was the anxiety expressed about a society in seeming moral and genetic decline.

Just 3 years after the publication of this text, the geneticist R. C. Punnett rebuked eugenicists for believing that recessives could be easily eliminated in just a few generations through breeding programs (Punnett, 1917, pp. 464–465). While we cannot make Hunter responsible for knowing of these findings in 1914, we can expect that his later volumes would reflect these changes. They did not.

The majority of the texts in this analysis included discussions of the destructive inherited traits of the Jukes and the Kallikak families. They were compared in turn with superior family types whose qualities were also judged hereditary. Hunter included similar lists, pointing out that socially prominent members of the patrician Edwards family could "trace the characters which enabled them to occupy the positions of culture and learning they held" back to the matriarch of the family, Elizabeth Tuttle. In the parlance of the day he concluded that "blood tells" (Hunter, 1914, p. 264). Yet in 1914 he was not an extreme eugenicist; his text accepted the possibility of "euthenics," or environmental reform, as well as eugenics.

New Civic Biology: Presented in Problems (1926), G. W. Hunter

Hunter's commitment to social efficiency and education continued with the 1926 *New Civic Biology: Presented in Problems*, which featured Clarence

Kingsley's well-known Seven Cardinal Principles. The Kingsley report strongly recommended a vocational rather than a civic orientation to American education policy. There is, of course, nothing wrong with articulating the legitimate links between biological knowledge and social policy in textbooks. Making these connections is appropriate if the data drive the policy and not the other way around. For example, many of these early science textbooks correctly warned their rural readers about the need for safe drinking water, cautioning them not to build their privies above their wells on hillsides. An understanding of gravity, germ theory, illness vectors, and water tables serves as the necessary empirical basis for this policy. Here the data inform the privy-building activity.

But today's readers should be aware that linking biological knowledge and social efficiency has often led to the capturing of genetic knowledge for particular political ends. When the connection between genetics and social policy is reversed; when an a priori commitment to human breeding takes priority over scientific understanding, then genetics can be distorted. Such a reversal seems to have occurred in Hunter's 1926 volume.

By 1926 the discussion of euthenics had been reduced from 24 pages to one, with a corresponding increase in the attention given to eugenics. "Choosing a vocation" was integrated into the discussion of inherited traits, and the text strongly implied that careful identification of these traits was required if efficient social location was to be based on biological merit. Repeating the charge of 12 years earlier, Hunter reminded his readers that "blood does tell!" and that although "life is made up of social inheritance, or what we *learn* through our *environment* . . . no one becomes great unless he or she has a nervous system of superior capacity" (Hunter, 1926, pp. 401–403, emphasis in original).

As with the 1914 edition, reports of the infamous Jukes and Kallikak and the desirable Edwards families were presented as examples to the text's 10th-grade readers as they confronted vocational and matrimonial choices. However, he instructed,

> Two applications of . . . [eugenics] stand out for us as high school students. One is the choice of a mate, the other is the choice of a vocation. As to the first, no better advice can be given than the old adage, "Look before you leap." If this advice were followed, there would be fewer unhappy marriages and divorces. Remember that marriage should mean love, respect, and companionship for life. The heredity of a husband or a wife counts for much in making this possible. (Hunter, 1926, p. 401)

Having underscored the importance of heredity in human relations, the discussion moved to its conclusion. The readers were told,

> Even though you are in high school, it's only fair to yourselves that you should remember the responsibility that marriage brings. You should be parents. Will you choose to have children well born? Or will you send them into the world with an inheritance that will handicap them for life? (p. 401)

Since neither amniocentesis nor genetic screening was available in 1926, no direct human genotypical observations could have been made in vitro. Hunter had to make his analysis of the phenotype, of the consequence of the dialectic of germ cells *and* environment through time. Simply put, he could not identify inheritance as a single factor. While today's medical geneticists can identify an increasing number of single-gene medical abnormalities that will undoubtedly impact on a fetus's postpartum existence, the *New Civic Biology's* references to the Kallikaks and Jukeses supplied no such genetic information. A belief in a particular social policy had preceded the science of the case. In these textbooks, ideology had distorted genetics.

Problems in Biology (1931)

Hunter's third text, *Problems in Biology*, was published in 1931 and while euthenics is now missing from the index, the categories of personal, family, and community hygiene are well covered. Reflecting changes in the biology of Hunter's day, the text moderates earlier observations, noting that "this mechanism of heredity is not as simple as it seems" (Hunter, 1931, p. 628). While blood was still important, it was now "chromosomes [that told] the story" (p. 639). Recognizing that programs of selective breeding might have little scientific support, Hunter explained that "it is clear that experiments which will attempt to separate and make new characters appear in the offspring will be extremely difficult, to say the least" (p. 638). And quoting H. S. Jennings, he notes that the "'characteristics that are predictable are extremely few' [and] we are finding out that our problems of breeding are not as easy as we had first hoped" (p. 629). Despite these caveats, the general discussion of phenotypic improvement did not change significantly from his earlier texts. One still hears the litany of the loathsome Jukeses and Kallikaks, and the desirable Edwards. One still learns that competence runs in families. And one still finds that wise choices in marriage and vocation are driven by the imperative of biology.

Science in Our World of Progress (1935)

Hunter's fourth volume, co-authored with W. G. Whitman, was published in 1935. *Science in Our World of Progress* was designed for the student of the then-emerging junior high school. Its focus was on an integration of science subject matter "written from the pupil viewpoint" (Hunter & Whitman, 1935, p. viii). While the volume identified environmental change as a useful venue for reform—"through personal hygiene and improvement of the environment, a healthier and stronger race has been produced"—the reader was still warned not to disregard heredity. "If we study . . . certain well-known families in this country who have become a burden to society," the authors warned, "we find that breeding in man . . . must be taken into account" (p. 483). And who were these families in 1935? They were the now-familiar Kallikaks and Jukeses. Do not accept simplistic environmental explanations for their criminal and depraved behaviors, the authors warned their ninth-grade readers, "it is not environment that always causes crime anymore than it is environment which always conditions an individual's life" (p. 483).

Attributing the cause of crime to inherited feeblemindedness, Hunter and Whitman (1935) recommended programs of segregation and sterilization, pointing favorably to "Germany [which has] laws which allow such persons to be sterilized or rendered incapable of reproduction" (p. 483). While a more intensive analysis of those laws would have revealed their political motivations, the authors included little of this background in their recommendations. They continued to put forward the examples of the Edwards and Roosevelt families, "which show that blood will tell, or rather to put it more scientifically, 'that chromosomes will tell the story'" (p. 483). Whether by blood or chromosomes, theirs was a story of biological determinism, whose litany ran, "if the race is to be improved, we must improve the stock . . . [and] the science of improving the human race by better heredity is known as *eugenics*" (p. 486, emphasis in original). Once again, with the exception of the few single-gene defects known at that time, little was understood about the genetic basis for human improvement and Punnett's (1917) caveat was very much in effect.

That Hunter and Whitman could have known much more about the political uses of eugenics in Germany in 1935 is another issue. The most generous observation that one can make today is to assume that the authors were both uncritical and naive about the social abuses of genetics. While such naiveté does not make them culpable for the German misuse of science, it surely makes them less than the best choices for authoring textbooks for adolescents.

Having favorably reviewed those policies of negative eugenics, they moved to positive eugenic proposals. "We must do all we can," they counseled their readers, "to have persons of the better stock mate and have children" (Hunter & Whitman, 1935, p. 483). This was an issue with overtones of international competition. "If this country is to succeed," they warned, "we must have brains and ability handed down to the next generation" (p. 483). Such a program of planned breeding was already in existence in Europe at the time; established by Heinrich Himmler with assistance of the Nazi SS, the program was called *Lebensborn*—The Well of Life. As European Holocaust historian Lucy Dawidowicz (1975) notes, the program's "ultimate goal ... was to form a racially superior stock from which Germany's future leadership would come" (p. 74). The authors of *Science in Our World of Progress* made no comment about that program.

Life Science: A Social Biology (1941)

Hunter's 1941 text, *Life Science: A Social Biology*, presents the most straightforward articulation of the eugenical themes he had developed during the previous 27 years. "Suppose," he queries his readers, "that we can change the physical makeup of a plant or an animal through some outside agency, is it possible to change our mental inheritance [as well]?" (Hunter, 1941, p. 766). While environment must be considered, the scales were tilted toward the determinism of heredity. "The important factor to remember," he pointed out, "[is that] there is no real evidence that the environment changes the intelligence of people."

> Those of low-grade intelligence would do little better under the most favorable conditions possible, while those of superior intelligence will make good no matter what handicaps they are given. (p. 759)

The political message embedded in this conclusion is direct. Social theorists who were arguing for a welfare state were wasting their time and would waste the resources of the nation. The inevitability of biology, as presented in almost three decades of Hunter's textbooks, made such a policy irrational. Biological science required a laissez-faire social policy for social services, and a centrally controlled policy for human procreation.

By 1941, despite more than two decades of scientific findings indicating that a simple hereditarian interpretation of human improvement was unwarranted, Hunter continued to teach students that "heredity was the basis upon which success in life is dependent," and that eugenics, "the science of being well born, or born well, healthy, and fit in every way," was the legitimate scientific basis for a worthy social policy. Indeed, 8 years after the Nuremberg Laws had been passed in Germany, Hunter described eugenics in the following fashion: "[Eugenics] means that we should make a real effort to separate those who are socially, physically, and morally fit from those who are not." The solution, in his view, was to institute a program of eugenics that would allow "only the fit to hand down their traits to their offspring" (Hunter, 1941, p. 760). But Hunter was to despair for such a possibility because American democratic traditions resisted such policies. "Such a . . . [program of negative eugenics]," he lamented in 1941, "is impossible with the present standards of society, but when we realize what has occurred through the breeding of bad stocks, we are shocked and alarmed" (p. 760).

While we have no evidence that he influenced public standards directly, Hunter did test his readers—the correct answers are italicized.

> To make matters worse, the feebleminded are breeding much faster than the *mentally* fit. To meet this situation, it is necessary to have some *physical* control, thus preventing this kind of person from breeding. Two methods, one *segregation* into separate institutions for males and females, the other *sterilization* or prevention of breeding are possible practices. A third is by practicing *eugenics*, by having those of good physical constitutions and *mental* ability marry and have children. (Hunter, 1941, p. 767)

We should realize that this examination did not represent good science. By 1941, the proposition that the inheritance of mental ability was a simple matter of breeding best with best, regardless of social context, was outside the mainstream of biological thought. Yet this was Hunter's position. And in order to reinforce that belief, the text repeats the eugenically popular dictum for its student readers: "Wooden legs are not inherited but wooden heads are" (p. 772).

Even the rapidly spreading European war had eugenical possibilities for George William Hunter. Years after Popenoe and Johnson had ceased to suggest it, he argued that "a good biologist would . . . [send] the mentally unfit to be killed off and [keep] the biologically fit at home to continue the race" (Hunter, 1941, p. 772).

Yet Hunter did not seem pleased with what he had learned from his discipline after 27 years of authoring biology textbooks for adolescents. With America's involvement in war fast approaching, he concluded that the least able should be sacrificed, but that an uninformed public would do nothing to resist the eugenic waste.

How the young readers of Hunter's texts responded to these social messages is obviously beyond the scope of this analysis. But the messages surely must be seen as part of their academic environment. Common themes tied the books together. They included commitments to the instrumental value of biology, to social efficiency in the form of a meliorative approach to social problems, and to the dominance of heredity over environment in the form of eugenics.

Biology in Human Affairs (1941)

Another high school biology textbook published in 1941 was John Woodside Ritchie's *Biology in Human Affairs*. Maintaining a commitment to biological determinism, this textbook is an early example of what would become known as the Life Adjustment approach to curriculum design. Focusing on the theme of adjustment, Ritchie advises his readers on the importance of the biological sciences.

> Biology, more than any other science . . . teaches us to understand ourselves. This helps us to see ourselves as we are, to perceive what we can and cannot do and to concentrate on what we can change and improve. (Ritchie, 1941, p. 31)

And when the case is that most elusive quality, individual human intelligence, change is well beyond our capacities. "We do not fight against gravity, because it is no use, we are resigned to the succession of the seasons because we know we cannot stop them" (p. 31). Ignoring such realities can only lead to personal dissatisfaction. "When we understand the world and our own [intellectual] abilities," he explained, "we tend to give up impossible hopes and ambitions and to seek that which is possible for us" (p. 31). Ritchie's scientific authority for these recommendations was an allegedly deterministic biology. "The only wise course," he counseled his students, "is to bow to nature's authority, learn her laws, and live in harmony with her decrees. An understanding of biology," he concluded, "helps us see this and to do the things that nature will approve" (p. 31).

There were social policy implications for the readers' lives in this deterministic vision. For example, it appeared that nature did not approve of social programs guaranteeing equal opportunity to all. Highlighting differences in human intelligence, artistry, industry, unselfishness, and honesty, Ritchie argued that any policy that would increase social opportunity would only exacerbate social inequality. "Those with the best abilities profit most by opportunity and . . . the biologist . . . [appreciates] that the giving of freedom for the development and use of these abilities magnifies these differences" (Ritchie, 1941, p. 40). But no specific social order is required by the reality of human differences. That recommendation was Ritchie's. To his contemporaries who might have argued for a society of equal outcomes, he responded that such suggestions ignored the fixed laws of biology. If one wanted "to secure equality of accomplishment in any field of endeavor," he explained, "'the more efficient must be shackled that they not outrun the less efficient'" (p. 40). Yet neither a "shackled society" nor a society of equal outcomes follows from a study of human differences. Such social relations flow from ethical analyses and visions of social justice, not from biology. Ritchie's justification for an unequal society came not from his understandings of biology but from his political commitments.

As noted earlier in this chapter, the majority of the books in this review supported programs of selective human breeding and more than 63% of the texts supported eugenic marriage selection. Ritchie's volume is among that number. He instructed his readers: "The positive part of the program is the arranging of a social order that will allow and encourage those of high abilities and desirable character to marry early and raise large families" (Ritchie, 1941, p. 699). In 1941, programs of both positive and negative eugenics were recommended for adolescent consideration. "As you take your place . . . as citizen[s]," he pointed out, "you will be called upon to consider one social and political measure after another." In the political arena, where claims for nature and nurture competed, Ritchie suggested that limited attention be given to environmental reform. "Scan each measure from the point of view of whether it will in the end give us a citizenry with better or poorer genes," he warned, for "the welfare of a people in the end is determined by what the people are" (p. 699).

Once again, few single-gene diseases were recognized in 1941, and the genetic basis for complex human social behavior was, as it is today, unresolved. There was simply no way for Ritchie to unambiguously identify these "better" genes; he was limited to phenotypic proxies for this genetic substrate. He had to assume that persons of good character had good character genes, which were lacking in those of poor character. This presumption was without a biological warrant in 1941. It remains without substance to this day.

Biology and Human Welfare (1924)

Having considered two texts published in 1941, we return to the mid-1920s and to *Biology and Human Welfare*, written in 1924 by James Peabody and Ellsworth Hunt. It was not until this volume's last chapter, "How Success in Life is Won," that the authors discussed eugenics. Combining aphorisms for hard work with the stories that "like produces like" and that just as "race horses are descended from other race horses, it is blood that tells, in . . . human beings" (Peabody & Hunt, 1914/1924, p. 542), the chapter depicted a world in which social roles were biologically determined. Attempting to keep their readers from drawing the logical conclusion that in such a preordained world freedom is a myth, the text quickly turned to a discussion of nature and nurture. Here the high schoolers were presented with a two-part strategy for negotiating life's future challenges: "Improved environment and training may better the generation already born," they were told, so work hard. But since "improved blood will better every generation to come," a useful strategy would be to "marry and breed well" (p. 543). This was an interesting if somewhat contradictory message to offer to high school students. You are determined by your heredity, *Biology and Human Welfare* seems to tell its readers, but this is not a reason to despair; you do have a place in this complex society. If you keep your expectations modest, work hard, and marry well, you will do your part to improve the future. In some ways this is a story of delayed gratification rationalized in eugenic terms.

Peabody and Hunt's text also includes the requisite stories of superior and inferior family lines. As in the other volumes, high school students who could trace their heritage to those superior families would have a competitive advantage over their fellows. This point was underscored when the text explained that the Edwards's descendants "may be proud that such blood flows in [their] veins, for it is probably true that no other family has contributed more to our national welfare than [the Edwards]" (Peabody & Hunt, 1914/1924, p. 547). Here we see biology prefiguring political and economic relations. Policy, it would seem, depends less on knowledge of the nation's *political* constitution than on its "best" people's *biological* constitution.

But what was society to do with those judged constitutionally inferior? Here Peabody and Hunt (1914/1924) had a direct answer: Eliminate them. Only "a few generations . . . would be required," they explain, "to eliminate from human society the feebleminded and socially diseased . . . through a program of institutionalization and segregation" (p. 546). In the meantime, students should choose their mates carefully and demand detailed records from them. "Certain it is," the authors advise, "that every right-minded individual should avoid marrying into a family in which there is ancestral feeblemindedness and who . . . cannot furnish physical and mental health certificates signed by reliable physicians" (p. 543). For those wondering about the source of such recommendations, the authors were quick to identify "a great movement . . . known as Eugenics," which instructs that "any permanent improvement of the human race can only come as a result of better heritage" (p. 548).

Having thus outlined their vision of the primary importance of heredity in human betterment, Peabody and Hunt might well have received the complaint from their high school readers that lives were predetermined. "Why should we bother to work so hard if so much of our future is dependent on our unchangeable biological inheritance?" they might ask. Peabody and Hunt addressed the dilemma of a seemingly preordained future: Yes, they admitted, even though "enough has been said to show the tremendous consequences that come from good and bad heritage" such findings did not apply to the majority of their readers. "Most of us," they explained,

> belong to the great middle class in which heritage is neither exceptionally good nor strikingly bad. For this reason, in order to win success, each one of us must do all in his power to make . . . environment and response count for all that they are worth. (Peabody & Hunt, 1914/1924, p. 542)

Once again the social message is clear. Have modest goals, work hard, and do not expect significant social change. While the authors agreed that education is important, they viewed schooling as a rather anti-intellectual endeavor:

> Education is something more than going to school for a few weeks each year, [it] is more than knowing how to read and write. [Education] . . . has to do with character, with industry, and with patriotism. (p. 549)

Character, industry, patriotism; surely these are worthy dispositions. But they do not reflect the sort of critical habits of mind that might lead to social reformation. This is not the kind of education that would foster critical analysis. It is one that would support the social prescriptions of the authors.

In conclusion, it would not be difficult for the readers of this text to anticipate their futures based on the above discussion. For descendants of the Edwards's class, the future held promise for continued contributions to the "national welfare" (Peabody & Hunt, 1914/1924, p. 547). For the offspring of the Jukeses and the Kallikaks, a life of institutionalization awaited, where they would be "prevented from transmitting to other generations their physical, mental, and moral weaknesses" (p. 546).

But what of the majority of the readers? What of those middle-class students of allegedly middling heritage? What sort of life could they look forward to? Using a gendered vocabulary typical of the times, Peabody and Hunt (1914/1924) explain that theirs would be a life of hard work and perseverance leading to equally middling ends. "If he keeps faithfully busy each hour of the day," Peabody and Hunt advise, "he may safely leave the final result to itself. [The middle-class student] can with perfect certainty count on waking up some fine morning to find himself one of the competent ones of his generation in whatever pursuit he may have singled out" (p. 552). The acute student could easily read one of three possible social trajectories from the text's eugenic tale: excellence, competence, or institutionalization.

Animal Biology (1948)

An examination of this last volume demonstrates how successfully eugenics had been promoted by the late 1940s. *Animal Biology*, written by the well-known University of Wisconsin biologist Michael F. Guyer, was published in 1948, and introduced eugenics early in the first chapter as "a subject upon which the very perpetuation of our civilization depends" (Guyer, 1948, p. 14). In the context of a progressive concern for the nation's natural resources (forests, pollution, food inspection, vaccination, quarantine, hunting and fishing restrictions), Guyer recommended carefully guarding the genetic resources of the people as well. Animal and plant breeders, the reader is informed, can predict and control future generations and the same was true for humans:

> In his various strains of plants and animals . . . [the geneticist] can often combine desirable characters and eliminate undesirable ones. And it is now known that human structures and aptitudes, whether they make for man's weal or woe, are subject to the same laws. (p. 15)

They were laws that individuals ignored at their peril. They demanded action of an informed citizenry. "In brief," the high school reader is informed, "such definite advances in our knowledge of the processes of human heredity are being made that we can no longer refuse to take up the social duties which the facts thrust upon us" (p. 15). Making the eugenicists' traditional points that ability ran in families (and must therefore be hereditary), that inborn inequalities would not be equalized by training, that nature is far more important than nurture in human performance, Guyer argued, as had Ritchie 7 years earlier, that education should maximize hereditary differences.

Here again, the rationale for eugenics was a corporate rather than an individualistic one. While individuals might benefit from eugenical social policies and practices, it was the interests of the collective and policies of differential birthrates that were Guyer's primary concerns. The eugenicist, he proclaimed,

> stresses the desirability of producing more individuals who are endowed by heredity with good physical and mental attributes, and fewer who are constitutionally inferior. . . . He maintains, that the question of breed—of natural endowment—is of fundamental importance to his nation. (Guyer, 1948, p. 552)

The similarity between Guyer's observations and those of the earliest biology text in this review are striking. "Certain hereditary types," he concluded, "are more valuable to society and the race than others . . . [and] in many family strains the seeds of derangement and disability have become so firmly established that they menace the remainder of the population" (p. 555). In a paragraph that reduced democracy to a biological problem, Guyer warns that "a successful democracy can in last analysis spring only from good blood." For Guyer, society's less worthy members represented a clear and present danger to the nation's future. Sounding much like the early 20th-century racist, Madison Grant, Guyer observed that at present the less able fourth of our population is producing approximately one-half of the next generation. The greatest danger to any democracy is that its abler members and less prolific types shall be swamped by the overproduction of inferior strains. This has been the fate of past civilizations—why not America? (p. 556)

Guyer (1948) used the terms and categories of his predecessors to demand that we "take our own evolution in hand and deal with our four chief menaces." These included (1) the dysgenic effects of war; (2) an "unwise charity which fosters the production of unfit strains"; (3) the "immigration of individuals with inferior mentality and ability"; and (4) the relative infertility of "superior stocks" (p. 556). Echoing Franklin Bobbitt, a pioneer in the field of curriculum policy, Guyer warned that natural selection was not operating naturally. "Inferior stocks are not only holding their own, but some are increasing faster than good stocks" (p. 557). Directed at just these good stocks, the text recommended a program of applied eugenics.

In tones more melancholy than scientific, Guyer concluded that "unless we can institute an intelligent personal selection in place of the natural selection which we are thwarting, the prospect for our nation—for civilization as a whole, indeed—is far from encouraging" (p. 557).

CONCLUSION

For those who would argue that eugenics was rejected by members of the educational community after the 1920s and therefore had no significant impact on the curriculum, these textbooks stand as powerfully disconfirming evidence. While it is certainly true that by the late teens geneticists had rejected models that directly applied genetics to the manipulation of complex human qualities, their rejection seems to have had little effect on the textbooks under examination in this chapter. Whether by consequence of what one might call a "dissemination lag" or by intention, the majority of the books did not report the conceptual and empirical changes under way in biology at the time. While not mirroring the genetic developments of the period, they did reflect a series of status quo–oriented social policies.

Indeed, most of these eight books reflected social attitudes and political theories rather than a clear rendering of scientific data. As this analysis has shown, the texts' commitment to a hierarchical and corporate social order that assigned individuals social locations based on their hereditary worth preceded and informed their discussion of human possibilities. Beginning in the middle-teens, and certainly by the 1920s, the majority of the texts' views on eugenics were no longer reflective of mainstream biological science.

Today we expect social issues to be presented in textbooks as problems needing to be confronted and resolved. Such problems require our best scientific and ethical reasoning. Today we find curriculum policy that values social responsibility as one of the criteria for selecting textbooks. Educators now ask whether the content of a science text is "likely to help citizens participate intelligently in making social and political decisions on matters involving science and technology" (Rutherford, 1989, p. 21). As we have seen in this analysis, these early biology texts did not meet that standard. When the issue was improving humankind through programs of selective breeding, they did not help their readers to participate intelligently in matters involving science and technology. They presented one answer from a broad array of possibilities rather than supplying their readers with evidence to facilitate their problem solving. While mainline eugenics is generally rejected today in the academic community, our responsibility to speak truth to power remains. It requires that we maintain "a healthy balance . . . between openness and skepticism" (Rutherford, 1989, p. 135).

We now recognize that such habits of mind were missing from the leadership of American Eugenics during the early 20th century. That such skeptical attitudes were similarly absent from these science textbooks suggests that eugenics did indeed have an important and negative impact on the American school curriculum through the late 1940s.

Having traced eugenics from its organizational roots through its popularization to its influence on the school textbook, we turn now to its impact on more general curricular policies. The chapter that follows will trace the influence of eugenics on policies for the classification of students with exceptionalities in the 1920s and 1930s.

CHAPTER 5

Biological Determinism and Exceptional Students

Stupidity begets stupidity, and intelligence begets brains, but a thousand years of educating or improving the parents will never improve the children. If that is all you do it is highly probable that you will deteriorate the children into extinction. This is because the children are born not from the improved body cells but from the unimproved germ cells. Children are born not from the body and brain cells which you can educate, but from the germ cells, which by any process now known you cannot educate. In short, statesmanship should quickly learn the lesson of biology, as stated by Conklin, that "Wooden legs are not inherited, but wooden heads are."
—A. E. Wiggam, The New Decalogue of Science, 1923

Only a small minority of children testing in the highest group for intellect, originate among the manual workers in cities, in the United States (where the social-economic competition is relatively free for all). There are various possible interpretations of this fact, but the inference most favored by all subsidiary facts is that the very intelligent are those who rise in the world by competition, and who are also able to produce children like themselves. In fact, it has been proved again and again that ability "runs in families."
—Leta S. Hollingworth, "Provisions for Intellectually Superior Children,"
The Child: His Nature and His Needs, 1924

This chapter focuses on the relationship between the desire of eugenics for social efficiency and the developing field of mental measurement in the early 20th century. It highlights the links between eugenics and policies of student classification. We begin our analysis with a consideration of the quotations that introduce the chapter. Their authors had quite different professional careers: Albert E. Wiggam was a vulgar popularizer of eugenics, while Leta Hollingworth was a respected professor of education. Despite these differences, they shared a number of basic assumptions about human development and social policy. They both assumed that it was human inheritance, in either germ cells or genes, that was the dominant if not the exclusive factor in understanding and predicting human action. Although the potential for all human behavior is inherited, this inheritance is immediately enfolded, in a nonseparable fashion, into a human non-biological context; that is, the human genotype is immediately enfolded into human culture. In an important sense then, human beings are no more determined exclusively by their biology than they are determined solely by their cultural context. The dialectic of human development is instead revealed in the interplay between biological and cultural possibilities.

While we will not return to a contemporary analysis of these issues until Chapter 7, for readers attempting to make sense of today's debates surrounding intelligence and its measurement, the concept of possibility can be a powerful analytic construct. This notion of possibility will have to be critically applied to the determinist views that tied the work of Wiggam and Hollingworth together.

In his eloquent critique of determinist thinking, *The Mismeasure of Man*, Stephen Jay Gould (1981) warns that "biological determinism is, in its essence, a *theory of limits*. It takes the current status of groups as a measure of where they should and must be even while it allows some rare individuals to rise as a consequence of their fortunate biology" (p. 28, emphasis in original). The history of American Eugenics has more often than not been a history of the categorization of individuals and groups for the purpose of legitimating a set of existing social, institutional, and political relations.

In the United States in the 1920s for example, the concept of differential racial or biological worth was not merely a curiosity of the academy; it had direct political consequences. As we have seen in earlier chapters, this belief gave legitimacy to policies of racial discrimination, immigration restriction, and sterilization. This chapter focuses on the ways in which notions of biological determinism were transformed, refined, and developed as a basis for public policies for institutionalized members of society, whether in hospitals, prisons, or schools. An understanding of these practices and of the articulate spokespersons who offered them intellectual support in the 1920s is necessary for an understanding of the current debate concerning intelligence and its measurement.

ALBERT E. WIGGAM AND THE IMPERATIVE OF BIOLOGY

Many of the members of the American Eugenics movement authored best-selling volumes popularizing its policies and programs. In addition to the work of Grant, Davenport, and Popenoe and Johnson, a list of those volumes would have to include A. E. Wiggam's *The New Decalogue of Science* (1922). Wiggam was a member of the Eugenics Section of the central committee of the 1928 Race Betterment Conference along with C. B. Davenport, Albert Johnson, and H. H. Laughlin. Johnson was co-sponsor of the 1924 immigration restriction law, and Laughlin gave "expert testimony" to Johnson's committee.

Wiggam's volume, written in the form of testimony before an imaginary public official, outlined a causal relationship between biology and statesmanship. In a peculiar blending of religion and biology, Wiggam described a pattern of behavior beginning with the giving of the Ten Commandments and ending with the scientific discoveries of his day.

> What I think will surprise Your Excellency is that God is still doing the same thing. . . . [But] instead of using tables of stone . . . to reveal His will, He has given men the microscope, the spectroscope, the telescope, the chemist's test tube and the statistician's curve in order to enable men to make their own revelations. (Wiggam, 1922, pp. 17–18)

These "instruments of divine revelation," Wiggam's protagonist concluded, "have not only added an enormous range of new commandments—an entirely new *Decalogue*—to man's moral code, but they have supplied him with the technique for putting the old ones into effect" (p. 18). Despite this seeming optimism, Wiggam was anxious about the future of human improvement; "the advanced races of mankind are going backward," he warned, and "the civilized races of the world are biologically plunging downward." Citing a litany of presumably inherited characteristics, he despaired that imbeciles, weaklings, paupers, and hoboes were increasing in number while leadership and genius were on the decline (pp. 25–26). The evidence for this decrease in human quality was supplied in part by two leaders in the field of mental testing, Edward L. Thorndike and Robert M. Yerkes.

While it is important to recognize that intelligence is a socially constructed category and its "heritability" is therefore problematic in the extreme sense, the notion that the categories of pauper and hobo were heritable was problematic even in the 1920s. The desire to cleanse society of imbeciles may be seen charitably as the workings of an immature intellect, but the desire to remove pauper germ plasm or unit characters from the population is not. This latter policy is better seen as the workings of social animus toward those with lower-class behaviors. It had no empirically valid basis by the 1920s; it was not science.

For Wiggam, like Bobbitt and others before him, the villains of the piece were civilization and race differences. "After making all possible allowances," he explained, the "biologist gains a strong impression from . . . mental testers that one of the outstanding results of civilization is that it has made the world safe for stupidity" (Wiggam, 1922, p. 31). Do not meddle with human progress he warned, unless you are willing to take control. "Evolution is a bloody business [and while] civilization tries to make it a pink tea . . . [it] is the most dangerous enterprise upon which man ever set out" (p. 34). And repeating points made in many of the science textbooks we reviewed in Chapter 4, Wiggam cautioned that danger lurks in differential birthrates that do not favor an increase in the progeny of the nation's leaders. Differential birthrates, he explains, existed in the past, but the development of civilization has taken "man out of the bloody, brutal but beneficial hand of natural selection [and] . . . placed him at once in the soft perfumed, dainty gloved but far more dangerous hand of artificial selection. Call science to your aid," Wiggam demanded of the statesman in the *New Decalogue*, "and make this artificial selection as efficient as the rude methods of nature [or else you will] bungle the whole task. And you are doing this on a colossal scale in industrial America" (p. 34). The text then took a rather nasty racial turn as he complained that society had "deliberately introduced within the past two decades, at least two million oppressed people of other lands, of lower intellectual ability than your . . . negroes already on hand" who were a threat themselves "since mixed races are a menace in the operation of popular government" (p. 35). This victim-blaming strategy has always been a ploy of the racist. Disregarding social constraints on the achievement of minorities as a class or group, Wiggam toured the country disseminating the scientifically unwarranted story that "biological" or "evolutionary" factors require the exclusion or repression of racial minorities (Figure 5.1).

Six decades ago, A. E. Wiggam used just such arguments to depict immigrants and in-migrants as a national threat to America's Nordics and their inborn qualities of mental alertness, social cohesiveness, and political capacity. His assumptions about the differences between Nordics and Negroes were based on Carl C. Brigham's 1923 work, *A Study of American Intelligence*. As noted earlier, this popular text found hierarchies of racial worth legitimated by the differing performance levels of ethnic groups on the American Army Alpha and Beta tests. While Brigham himself would eventually recant and reject these racial interpretations, the damage was done; racism had been given scientific legitimation. For many Americans during this period, the Army Alpha and Beta test data, as well as the popular texts by Wiggam and Brigham, helped to reinforce the "facts" of a racial hierarchy (Selden, 1987).

ARMY ALPHA AND ARMY BETA:
MEASURING THE IMPERATIVE

Robert Yerkes wanted to establish the science of psychological measurement, still fairly new in 1917, as a professionally legitimate field. He thought

FIGURE 5.1. Albert E. Wiggam on Tour Discussing Eugenics and Civilization. Courtesy of the Lilly Library, Bloomington, Indiana.

he could do this, as well as assist in the war effort, by evaluating American recruits for the First World War. Yerkes approached the War Department with his plan, whose centerpiece was the development of a set of tests of military manpower. These exams, known as Army Alpha and Beta, were authored by a seven-person committee, which included among its membership the eugenicists H. H. Goddard, Lewis Terman, and Yerkes himself. As the committee members met to formulate the tests in the summer of 1917 at the bucolic setting of the Vineland Training School for Feebleminded Boys and Girls, they assumed they were developing tests to measure the innate intelligence of prospective enlistees. The Alpha and Beta nomenclature refers to the two forms of the test: Alpha was administered to literate recruits, Beta to those judged illiterate.

Gould (1981) has taken a critical look at the project. He notes that rather than evaluating innate intelligence, the tests were more than likely measuring the recruits' familiarity with American culture. Consider the following items, which were administered to both native-born and foreign literate recruits:

Christy Mathewson is famous as a:
    writer, artist, baseball player, comedian.
Crisco is a:
    patent medicine, disinfectant, toothpaste, food product.

> The number of a Kaffir's legs is:
>   two, four, six, eight. (p. 200)

As a devotee of the game, Gould knows quite well that Christy Mathewson was a baseball player. And I would imagine that most present-day readers would correctly identify Crisco as a food product. But the Kaffir inquiry poses a special problem. Kaffir when capitalized stands for a Bantu-speaking South African, while kaffir with a lower case *k* is a form of sorghum. The problem for the literate recruit who has learned of kaffir on the farm (recall that this is an Alpha item) is that none of these answers makes sense. After all, grasses have no feet.

I am not interested in becoming embroiled in an argument on item construction here. But it should be evident that when answers are based on culturally bounded information, they are not measures of innate intelligence. As Gould (1981) points out, it is not surprising that native-born Americans did better on the examination than did immigrants. Nor is it surprising that recruits who were schooled did better than those who were not.

Yet the test constructors were committed to the overriding importance of heredity in human intellectual development, and they believed that their items would measure innate intelligence, not the effects of environment. And so when Robert Yerkes learned that low scores on the examinations were highly correlated with ringworm infection, he offered an explanation in terms of inheritance. "Low native ability," he explained, "may induce such conditions of living as to result in hookworm infection" (Gould, 1981, p. 218). Gould argues most convincingly that the conclusions concerning racial differences drawn from the data were unwarranted and that the conditions of the test administration and the subsequent statistical analyses make the findings themselves a problematic basis for social or educational policy.

EQUAL OPPORTUNITY AS A REQUIREMENT FOR SOCIAL INEQUALITY

For Albert Wiggam, these same test data drove a set of self-evident social policies. To his mind, the test results required a program that would afford equal opportunity to all in order to create a society typified by inequality. Humankind, he observed, is "created unequal in all respects and leaders come not by prayer but by germ cells. The final test of democracy," he charged, "is its capacity to breed leaders" (Wiggam, 1922, p. 42). Using a rationale that should now be familiar to us, Wiggam argued that in a society where individuals have differing abilities, the offer of equal opportunity would lead to social inequality. Equal opportunity was not synonymous with the equality of outcomes. While there are some who find this argument compelling, it continues to suffer from the same limitations it did 60 years ago. Making it society's goal to maximize an individual's hereditary advantage is just as much a value choice as is maximizing the common good. It is not a necessary corollary of test-score differences. The argument that biological determinism prefigures an unequal "market society" in which individuals use their biological inheritance to compete for limited resources abuses science as well as ethics. Whether in the 1920s or today, arguments that human biological differences mandate social inequality are still illogical.

The social inequality that Wiggam found inevitable was based on a vision of immutable, hierarchical, biological inequality. Social policies that did not directly influence an individual's biological makeup were at best a waste of time and at worst a threat to society. The *New Decalogue*'s statesman was warned not to engage with such fruitless endeavors. "[The] social classes, therefore, which you seek to abolish are ordained by nature; that it is in the large statistical run of things, not the slums which make slum people, but slum people who make slums."

> That primarily it is not the Church which makes people good, but good people who make the church; that godly people are largely born and not made; that if you want church members you will have to give nature a chance to produce them; that if you want artists, poets, philosophers, skilled workmen and great statesmen, you will have to give nature a chance and breed them. (Wiggam, 1922, p. 43)

The belief that humankind was a product of its genetic inheritance, needing only programs of manipulation for improvement, was a central theme of the mainline eugenicists. And Wiggam's *New Decalogue of Science* was nothing if not mainline.

Like many Mendelian eugenicists of the period, Wiggam had his list of traits that were inherited in Mendelian ratios. It included "high temper, uncontrollable fits of anger, feebleness of will, inability to hold a social ideal permanently in mind, lack of ambition to provide as good homes as their neighbors, [and] . . . mental 'drive'" (Wiggam, 1922, p. 58). More specifically, he argued that high temper was a "pure 'dominant' inherited thing, like brown eyes and curly hair" (p. 59). In 1922, he concluded that both human behavior and social organization were predetermined by the iron laws of biological science. In summarizing the first new commandment of the *Decalogue*, he proclaimed that "had Jesus been among us, he would have been president of the First Eugenics Congress" (p. 110).

C. C. PETERS AND THE REQUIREMENTS
OF SOCIOBIOLOGY

A commitment to the idea of heredity as the primary maker of people also guided the work of one of America's leading educational sociologists, Charles C. Peters. Peters's *Foundations of Educational Sociology* (1930) was used extensively in teacher training in the 1930s and dealt directly with the role of the family in human betterment. The family, prospective teachers were informed, "can make its contribution to society on the selective side by insuring to the race well born children" (p. 273). Proposing, as had Wiggam, that democracy makes a "fetish" of equal opportunity, Peters implies that it is senseless to bring handicapped individuals full term as "they come into life with a drag" (p. 274). His list of heritable handicaps included "insanity, feeble-mindedness, nervousness, criminality, moral delinquency, physical malformations, weakness of personality, [and] susceptibility to disease" (p. 274).

Lest the reader view these qualities as a result of environmental influence, some prebirth trauma, or pure chance, Peters (1930) instructs that these traits "are no more accidents than is the collision of two trains" (p. 274). And these laws, he added, must be the engines for social policy.

Yet there was little scientific warrant during Peters's day for such policy prescriptions. As Cravens (1978) points out, "between the early 1900s and the late 1920s the most visible eugenics leaders recited the same interpretations of heredity, variation, and evolution."

> [Taking] scant notice of the momentous intellectual revolutions in the field of genetics in those years . . . [eugenicists] commonly argued that heredity was all powerful, [and] that environment was of little or no effect in man as in lower animals. . . . [They] commonly insisted that all human traits, mental and physical, were Mendelian unit characters in the germ plasm, were transmitted as independent, nonreducible characters, and constituted the basis for all traits, desirable and undesirable in man. (p. 46)

Peters held just such a position as he developed his own list of heritable qualities.

Note the reversal of attitudes between those we might have termed "liberal" or "conservative" in an earlier time. In 1930 it was liberal thinkers who argued that incontrovertible evidence did not exist to justify denying reproductive rights to individuals with unsatisfactory genetic inheritance. The conservative position, held by Peters, argued for restraint on the part of "carriers" of social and physical defects; they should terminate such pregnancies. Today, it is the liberal position that supports the mother's option to terminate such pregnancies. The conservative position, articulated in the United States by the Right to Life movement, demands full term for all fetuses, regardless of the mother's wishes, or for exceptionalities identified through fetal analysis. The element of the liberal position that has remained unchanged over 60 years is that the choice to bear a child must lie with the mother.

We err however, if we see these competing positions as either correct or incorrect. As Diane Paul (1995) notes, the history of eugenics tells at least two stories. When seen as a story of people with disabilities, decisions to terminate pregnancy are

> not benign simply because their agents are private citizens. Indeed, if we insist on absolute reproductive autonomy, we [will have to] accept the use of genetic technologies to prevent the birth of those who are unwanted for any reason: that they will be the "wrong" gender, or sexual orientation, or of short stature, or prone to obesity. (p. 135)

Peters's story, on the other hand, is more likely one of destructive state power, and it is clear that he was not reticent in recommending programs of negative eugenics in the 1930s. He concluded that "on the whole we know enough to make great remedial use of our knowledge. Under these circumstances it would seem inexcusable if we left matters of race reproduction to drag on and care for themselves just by accident" (Peters, 1930, p. 277). Fearful of what he saw as an increasing number of social defectives, Peters considered alternatives for their elimination: segregation, state-mandated regulation, sterilization. Each is rejected in turn. Individual segregation was too expensive; regulation was inefficient; and sterilization was deemed too politically difficult to enact. "To make of sterilization a eugenic measure," he reasons, "we would need to apply it to all who can transmit unfortunate traits to posterity, whether themselves defective or only carriers of defectiveness." But this was too emotional an issue for a reluctant public whose "sentiment would not yet sanction so comprehensive a program as a matter of legal compulsion" (p. 279). Peters's solution was a policy of voluntary sterilization before marriage. The specifics of his program were not to be found in the body of his text itself. They were located in a footnote describing the technique that will achieve sterility. "Although there has not yet been sufficient investigation of the matter," Peters explained "it seems probable that a still simpler effective method [to reduce exceptional individuals from future generations] is exposure to x-rays, which produce temporary sterility if the period of exposure is short and permanent if longer" (pp. 278–279).

While the secondary effects of such x-ray treatment may not have been known in 1930, the potential of negative eugenics for the elimination of recessive traits was understood by geneticists in Peters's day. That is, by 1930 the evidence supporting the elimination of traits such as feeblemindedness through such programs had been shown to be scientifically unattainable. As Ashley Montagu (1942) would point out a number of years later, one would have been deceived to believe that negative eugenics could be effective in easily eliminating undesirable characteristics from a population. "Were every feebleminded individual to be sterilized for the next two thousand years," Montagu observed, "the reduction in the number of feebleminded individuals in the population at the end of that time would not exceed 50 percent." And, he concluded with a wry sense of humor, "[that] is a very long time to have to wait for such a return" (p. 136). Furthermore, the cause of behaviors such as "criminality" or "moral delinquency" could be just as well searched for in the social context of those so afflicted as in their germ plasm. Social scientists gifted with Montagu's more dialectical view on human development might have found such social factors open to manipulation prior to the irreversible application of Dr. Roentgen's high-energy photons.

But Peters's eugenic commitments distorted his views on human improvement. Like his eugenical colleagues, he worried that society's best were not reproducing themselves rapidly enough. "There is no doubt," he lamented on the pages of *Foundations of Educational Sociology,*

> that the higher classes are, as a whole, shirking this responsibility for reasons of merely personal convenience. . . . There can be no doubt that certain undesirable classes impose a constant burden on society by reason of the prodigality with which they reproduce. (Peters, 1930, p. 280)

Once again, today's reader should be aware that in the absence of genetic evidence, "undesirable classes" remains a social category and not a biological one. While it is beyond the scope of this chapter to ascertain whether such distinctions were recognized by prospective teachers using Peters's text in the 1930s, it is clear that he believed that educational policy should be directed by the determinism of biology.

One additional example underscores Peters's hereditarian interpretations of human progress. By 1930, academics were well aware that correlations in and of themselves do not indicate causality. They were also aware that when a set of correlations supported contradictory hypotheses, any assumption as to the numbers' inherent meaning was problematic. As the following discussion will show, Peters seemed woefully unaware of these statistical constraints.

The section in *Foundations of Educational Sociology* concerned with methods of limiting the reproduction of "undesirable classes" included a table describing birthrate data for women in Vienna, Paris, and London. The table scaled women aged 15 to 50 years in terms of births per 1,000 and economic status (Figure 5.2).

One consistent relationship was reflected in the chart: Wealth and fecundity were inversely related. The richer you were, the fewer children you were likely to have. Peters recognized this relationship, placed it into his hereditarian world view, and concluded that while

> it does not, of course, follow that because certain parents are poor they are eugenically unfit; yet, on the whole, the fact that certain persons have ascended into the upper economic strata does show that they belong to strains capable of succeeding in the struggle of life. (Peters, 1930, p. 280)

Certainly this is true. But it is true of *all* who survived, not just the wealthy. One might even argue that Peters got it backward. For example, if one is to accept this analysis, then it is the poor, who outproduce the rich under difficult environmental circumstances, who embody the superior strains. In this interpretation, it would be the poor who were of superior ability; it would be the poor who have descended from better stock.

Peters (1930), however, made an a priori assumption that society's more fortunate were also its biologically superior. "It has been shown," he explained, "that the more fortunate social classes exceed the lower classes by as much as five inches in height on the average at certain ages and twenty pounds or more in weight, and that they exhibit in the mental tests a higher intelligence quotient." Identifying these differentials as biologically determined, he warned prospective teachers that "the greater fecundity among the lower classes does undoubtedly constitute a social problem" (p. 280).

The point of including this quotation is not to argue that all humans are equal in potential but rather to point out that Peters's (1930) assumptions about differential biological worth were cast in terms of class, not

	Very Poor	Poor	Well Off	Very Well Off	Rich	Very Rich
Paris	108	95	72	65	53	34
London	147	140	107	107	87	63
Vienna	200	164	155	153	107	71

FIGURE 5.2. Relation of Economic Status to Size of Family in Three European Cities. Number of Births per 1,000 Women Between Ages 15 and 50. (Based on Peters, 1930, p. 280)

biology. In his view, the lower classes were biologically less worthy than their exceptionally rich counterparts. The evidence? The fact that upper classes were taller, weighed more, and received higher scores on intelligence tests than their lower-class counterparts. Interestingly enough, Peters had to be both an environmentalist and a hereditarian to identify the lower classes as a social threat. As he made clear, only height, weight, and high IQ were heritable; fecundity varied inversely under the environmental pressure of wealth.

Given this inverse relationship between family size and economic status, a number of additional conclusions regarding the effect of the environment could have been drawn from the data. Peters could have surmised that, since Viennese women bore nearly twice as many children as their French counterparts, there was something in the environment that caused these women, regardless of economic status, to be more fecund. In any event, something in the location itself seems a significant factor. While I am not arguing that a vulgar environmentalism replace Peters's eugenic beliefs, it certainly seems reasonable to conclude that, once again, his hereditarian views predetermined the meaning he would make of empirical data.

HENRY H. GODDARD AND MANDATED STERILIZATION

As outlined in Chapter 1, the membership lists of eugenically oriented organizations often overlapped. For example, Wiggam was listed as a member of the Central Committee of the 1928 Race Betterment Conference, where he was joined by David Starr Jordan, Charles W. Eliot, and Henry Herbert Goddard. Jordan was president of Stanford University, Eliot was president of Harvard, and Goddard was the author of *The Kallikak Family: A Study in the Heritability of Feeble-Mindedness* (1912). All four shared membership in the Eugenics Society of America and the Eugenics Committee of the United States.

In addition to his central role in the popularization of eugenics, Goddard was a leader in the field of mental measurement in the United States. After receiving his Ph.D. in 1908, under the direction of the eugenicist G. S. Hall, Goddard went on to translate the Binet test for use with his students at the Training School at Vineland (New Jersey) for Feeble-Minded Girls and Boys. As the director of the school's research laboratory, he standardized the Binet on a population of southern New Jersey students. The test, which had been developed as a diagnostic device by Alfred Binet in France to assist student learning, took on a very different meaning in America. Armed with his North American findings, Goddard took to the lecture circuit, where he warned the nation of the threat of feeblemindedness and recommended programs of eugenics.

Summaries of his speeches were regularly featured in the local and national press. A 1913 Chicago presentation was reviewed in that city's papers as well as in those of Philadelphia, Baltimore, and Oskaloosa, Iowa. Recommending that "weak-minded" children be segregated by statute, he cast his lot with Wiggam. "It makes no difference" Goddard explained, "what phase of the problem of vice, drunkenness, pauperism or crime that we attack, we find feeble-mindedness in some form is the contributing cause" (*Oskaloosa Herald*, 1913, p. 1).

After Goddard addressed the Congress of Alienists and Neurologists, its Committee on Resolutions recommended that "any person that has been shown to be mentally unfit, and has been segregated because of same, he or she shall not be released from such segregation except under submitting to sterilization" (*Oskaloosa Herald*, 1913, p. 1). If society is plagued by prostitution and crime, segregate and sterilize the offenders and the problem will be eliminated. The committee further resolved that the "science of eugenics be incorporated in the regular curriculum of public high schools" (1913, p. 1). As we now know, this is exactly what happened. Whether it happened in direct response to this committee's recommendations or not, our earlier discussion of biology textbooks indicates that the majority of those books did indeed present eugenics as a legitimate science to their adolescent readers after 1913.

When Goddard wrote *The Kallikak Family* in 1912, he detailed the lineage of a "stock of paupers and ne'er-do-wells living in the pine barrens of New Jersey" (Gould, 1981, p. 168). These sad drains on the commonweal were created as a consequence of Martin Kallikak's dalliance with a feebleminded barmaid on his way to do battle in the American Revolution. From this unlawful union, Goddard reported on 480 descendants, of whom "one hundred and forty-three . . . were or are feeble-minded, while only forty-six have been found normal" (Goddard, 1912, p. 18). While the family may have been real, the Kallikak name was fictitious; it was created by Goddard's combining the Greek words for beauty (*kallos*) and bad (*kakos*). To make the hereditarian point more forcefully, Goddard noted that after the war Kallikak married a Quaker woman and that their progeny were all judged to be upstanding members of the community.

Figure 5.3 was taken from *The Kallikak Family*. It outlines the alleged Mendelian distributions of feeblemindedness and normalcy from Martin Kallikak's association with the "nameless feebleminded girl" and with his "lawful wife" (Goddard, 1912, p. 37). The Goddard text was filled with anecdotes on the lives of Kallikak's descendants. Included were charts

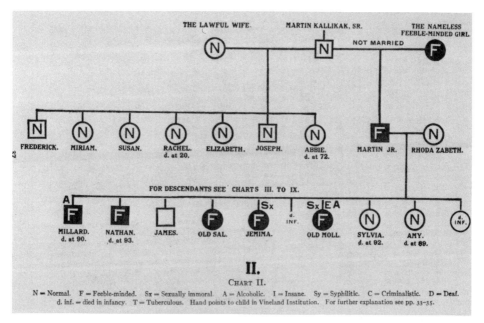

II.
Chart II.

N = Normal.   F = Feeble-minded.   Sx = Sexually immoral.   A = Alcoholic.   I = Insane.   Sy = Syphilitic.   C = Criminalistic.   D = Deaf.
d. inf. = died in infancy.   T = Tuberculous.   Hand points to child in Vineland Institution.   For further explanation see pp. 33–35.

FIGURE 5.3. Pedigree Chart Depicting Offspring from Martin Kallikak's Lawful Marriage and His Association with a Nameless Feebleminded Girl (1912). The letter "F" identifies feebleminded individuals. *The Kallikak Family: A Study in the Heredity of Feeble-Mindedness* (1912). The Macmillan Company.

depicting patterns of assumed Mendelian inheritance for feeblemindedness. In addition to anecdotes and charts, Goddard illustrated his point with retouched photographs of the then-living Kallikaks (Gould, 1981, pp. 171–177). In order to create a more menacing look among those identified by Goddard's field workers as "genetically afflicted," hairlines were changed, eyebrows were darkened, and mouths were made to turn down. There is no way to determine whether Goddard had any role in the misrepresentation of the visual facts. Regardless of its factual base, *The Kallikak Family* was an immensely popular book. It was used in educational psychology classrooms for decades after its publication and, as we have learned, it was cited in 25% of the high school biology textbooks of the period.

One photo that was not retouched (indeed its normal mien seems just the reason for its presence in Goddard's volume) was that of Deborah Kallikak (Figure 5.4). Judged to be a "high-grade moron," Deborah (and women like her) caused Goddard his deepest concern. Seemingly normal to the untrained eye, and obviously attractive, such a woman would have little trouble finding suitors and bearing children. And, of course, that was

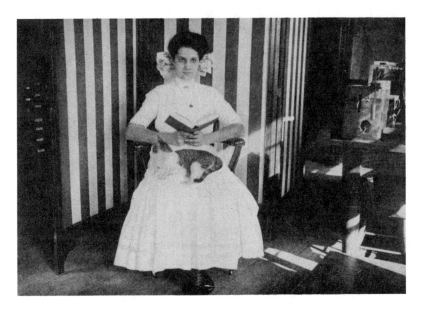

FIGURE 5.4. Deborah Kallikak as She Appeared in *The Kallikak Family: A Study in the Heredity of Feeble-Mindedness* (1912). The Macmillan Company.

the problem: Deborah's feebleminded taint would be passed on to another generation and the rising tide of feeblemindedness would continue unabated. The solution? Sterilization or segregation.

This fear of a "rising tide of feeblemindedness," as the threat was popularly called, continued to shape Goddard's social and educational policies, reappearing in his chapter in Michael V. O'Shea's *The Child: His Nature and His Needs*. Goddard (1924) proposed that differences in children require different educational and institutional responses. The foremost difference between children was that of their native intelligence. Yet too many educators incorrectly viewed children as essentially equal in intelligence. As a consequence, these teachers naively wasted valuable time and energy attempting to equalize that which was inherently unequal. Enlightened views on this subject were quite different, Goddard argued, and they were best summarized by the well-known eugenicist

> Henry Fairfield Osborn, who says the true spirit of American democracy, that all men are born with equal rights and duties has been confused with the political sophistry that all men are born with equal character to govern themselves and others . . . [and] with the educational sophistry that education and environment will offset the handicap of heredity. (p. 163)

These rather rash comments take on an even more disturbing connotation when we recall Osborn's role, along with that of Madison Grant, in organizing the racist Galton Society.

Judging the source of America's social burdens to be primarily biological, Goddard continued, "we have mistaken symptoms for causes. The cause of crime, insanity, and delinquency is not anything so simple as the movies, alcohol or any other numerous supposed causes. The cause is to be found in man's inherited tendencies" (Goddard, 1924, p. 174). By 1924 such a proposition had questionable genetic merit. Yet as historian of science Charles Rosenberg (1961) points out, "the more tenuous an area of scientific knowledge, the smaller its verifiable content, the more easily its data may be bent to social purposes" (p. 10). And while some educators might have found these hereditarian conclusions irrelevant to their work, Goddard continued to prescribe an active role for the schools, arguing that "the school must not lose sight of the fact that the making of good citizens is accomplished more successfully by teaching children to control their natural tendency to steal and to lie than by teaching them to read and write" (Goddard, 1924, p. 174). Given what we know today of the retouched photos in *The Kallikak Family* (Goddard, 1912), a concern for truth would indeed seem appropriate.

When Goddard wrote for *The Child: His Nature and His Needs,* Michael O'Shea was a professor of education at the University of Wisconsin; four years later O'Shea would join Wiggam on the Central Committee of the 1928 Race Betterment Conference. That powerful committee would also include University of Wisconsin President Glenn Frank; the nationally respected University of Chicago educator Charles Judd; the early curriculum leader W. W. Charters; and the famous muckraker of Standard Oil fame, Miss Ida Tarbell (Little, 1928a, pp. xxiv–xxv).

As with all references to membership lists, this information must be analyzed with the greatest of care, prior to judgment. Race Betterment was a progressive program that drew both liberal and conservative progressive support. While all progressives wanted to achieve human improvement, their means differed. In these differences one finds the distinction between a concern for human improvement through environmental change, on the one hand, and a concern for human betterment through hereditarian programming on the other.

In light of today's bioethical discourse regarding the Human Genome Project, it is important to recognize that neither a eugenic nor an environmental policy has a claim on the moral high ground. We are, after all, able to identify fetal gene defects today. Such a discovery might lead a woman to consider terminating the pregnancy of a Trisomy 21 (Down Syndrome) fetus. The ethical calculus of this decision would place a higher value on the potentially maximized independence of one future individual than on the more dependent existence of an individual with Down Syndrome. Or a mother might decide to bring the fetus to term regardless of the limitations on its postpartum existence. In this case the ethical presumption would be that a postpartum life, no matter how challenging the requirements for its full realization, is better than none at all. The first choice is, of course, the one that eugenicists of the 1920s would have supported. But we would be in error to confuse those earlier policies with those of the current scene. Today's bioethical decisions are based in part on an ethics of competing goods, which include serious consideration of human choice. The earlier policies were not. They limited freedom. They valued the state over the individual. And they reduced ethics to biology. Of greatest import, the eugenic policies of the 1920s were based on a profound misunderstanding of human genetics. Today, bioethical decisions on human reproduction are deeply informed by medical genetics and medical ethics. This is more than a difference of degree; it is a difference of kind.

LETA HOLLINGWORTH AND DIFFERENTIAL EDUCATION FOR THE GIFTED

The same volume that carried Goddard's chapter also included work by Leta S. Hollingworth (1924). Hollingworth, a professor at Teachers College, Columbia University, did not share Goddard's concern for the feebleminded. Recognized to this day as one of America's leading researchers and advocates for the education of the gifted child, she filled her chapter with references to Francis Galton, the founder of eugenics, and to issues raised by Wiggam and Peters. Presenting herself as a strong advocate of eugenics, she focused her readers' attention on the interests of the biologically meritorious, the group that she judges the citizenry's "best two per cent" (p. 279).

Hollingworth (1924) argued that social justice was a simple extension of the determinism of biology, and rejected the explanations of those who saw social inequalities in terms of economic inequalities. As Hollingworth explained it, society was already selecting individuals for social location based on their biological inheritance. The evidence for this assertion could be found in the background of very gifted children. These children, she explained, "originate in families where the father is a professional man, an owner or executive in business, or a clerical worker" (p. 290). Conversely, very few children from laboring classes were categorized in the highest group for intellect. Since the United States was a country where "the social-economic competition is relatively free for all," those who succeeded must have done so primarily as a consequence of inherited ability (p. 290). And this ability was presumably passed from successful parents to their children, who, in turn, achieved high scores on intelligence tests. Recognizing that there were various possible interpretations of these achievement data, Hollingworth concluded that "the inference most favored by all subsidiary facts is that the very intelligent are those who rise in the world of competition, and who are also able to produce children like themselves" (p. 290).

But not all was well in the policy arena when these children's interests were at stake. Educational policy, in Hollingworth's (1924) view, disregarded gifted children due to a misguided social philosophy that denied "innate permanent, hereditary superiority" (p. 299). A more effective policy would segregate these children into special classes. While few educators today accept Hollingworth's extreme position on the sources of exceptionality, there appears to be a schizoid policy at work for the treatment of the exceptional child. Some educational policies demand the mainstreaming of individuals at one extreme of the normal distribution while segregating those at the other. If a child has disabilities, this policy seems to say, bring these children into the classroom. On the other hand, if young persons are outliers in the upper percentiles of a standard measure, put those students into special classes in which they will be segregated by ability.

These ideas were expanded two years later in Hollingworth's well-known text on education for the gifted, *Gifted Children: Their Nature and Nurture* (1926). Consistent with her earlier observations that environment had little influence on individual development, Hollingworth found American society "preoccup[ied] with the incompetent" (p. vii). This concern was informed in part by the "natural tendency of human beings to notice whatever is giving them pain," and by a "wave of uninformed humanitarianism" (p. vii). These preoccupations were based on the false belief that social institutions could solve what was primarily a problem of heredity. Revealing a rather harsh view of the disabled, Hollingworth chided society for the construction of "expensive and even palatial institutes for the preservation and care of the feebleminded, the delinquent, the crippled, the insane, and others who varied biologically in the direction of social incompetence" (p. vii). Philanthropic efforts, she continued, "originally meaning love of man, degenerated to mean love of stupid and vicious man" (p. vii). Rejecting the idea that hereditary intelligence could be improved, she concluded that these philanthropic efforts were "actuated by the emotionally satisfying doctrine that all human beings are or might be born equal in merit; and that money, education, surgery, medicine and faith can eventually uplift any and all to the desired level of behavior" (p. vii).

Aware of environmentalist explanations for crime and underachievement, Hollingworth (1926) rejected them. "The facts do admit of a quite different explanation [than environmentalism]," she explains, "as has been clearly set forth by [the eugenicists] Galton, Pearson, Woods, Davenport, and Thorndike" (p. 12). As a scholar concerned for those students who scored highest on intelligence tests, Hollingworth knew of intellectual variation. But her answer to variation in human performance was at root an issue of differential inheritance:

> If children inherit their mental abilities through their parents, and if inherited ability is the prime determinant of achievement, then we shall expect to find almost all eminent persons to be born of parents above average in social status . . . [and whose] children will be born under the conditions they have wrought for themselves, or which they have inherited from their own parents, and that these children will be superior, as a group, if "like begets like." (p. 12)

Should one err and interpret the above conditions as though they were environmental factors leading to superiority, Hollingworth had an answer: "Opportunity and eminence are not causally related, except insofar as they are both referable to a common cause—able parents" (p. 12). As Hollingworth explained it, the lines of causality ran from parents to environment and from parents to offspring. Good environments did not account for superior student performance. Heredity, in Hollingworth's estimation, had won the day.

Today's reader might well ascertain that these comments are more than a half century old, and have little bearing on today's educational policies. The current literature on education for the gifted, however, belies this hypothesis. The general corpus of Hollingworth's (1926) work is still much cited. Of greater importance to this discussion, *Gifted Children: Their Nature and Nurture* continues to be cited in contemporary texts on giftedness. I would like to expand on this analysis because it sheds light on historical links between education for the gifted, eugenics, and the ways in which ethnicity has been framed historically in America.

Hollingworth (1926) linked intelligence and ethnicity, then went on to explain, in eugenic terms, differing performance levels between recent arrivals and settlers from an earlier period. She developed her argument by distinguishing between the quality of America's early settlers, "literate peoples who came here in the seventeenth century to a wild country, in order to obtain freedom for religious ideas" (p. 69), and more recent arrivals, such as Italians, who immigrated during the late 19th and early 20th centuries. She asserted that different groups immigrated for different reasons and the quality of these immigrant groups varied relative to their motives for immigration. In her view, 17th-century immigrants were worthy because they were "a very different sampling from the illiterate peoples who came here in the twentieth century, when the country was rich and prosperous, to earn money" (p. 69). These recent immigrants also seemed to produce a small number of gifted children. Even if there was a paucity of data concerning the proportion of gifted children by race and nationality in 1926, Hollingworth was able to cull one ethnically tinged finding from the studies. One "result . . . recurs persistently wherever American children are tested by nationality of ancestors," she emphasized. "American children of Italian parentage show a low average of intelligence. The selection of Italians received in this country has yielded very few gifted children" (p. 71). For some this would suggest meliorative interventions: better schools, improved language instruction, increased social services. But these interventions were not supported by Professor Hollingworth. "This inferiority," she explained by comparing ethnic groups with each other, "is not referable to 'language difficulty,' for children of Swedish and Jewish parentage . . . show a much higher average in the tests" (p. 71). As a trained psychologist, Hollingworth might have identified the cultural bias in tests that consistently revealed low intelligence by nationality. But as we have learned, she was a committed hereditarian, a supporter of eugenics: Little could be done environmentally to improve the lot of these underachieving children. Attempting change through social institutions would be meaningless or dysfunctional.

"Modern biology," she repeated in terms similar to those in her 1924 paper, "has shown that human beings cannot improve the qualities of their species, nor permanently reduce its miseries, by education, philanthropy, surgery, or legislation" (Hollingworth, 1926, p. 198). The answer was "eugenics . . . the art or technique of being well born," wherein "human beings could be reproduced for generations only from those who combine desirable qualities in the highest degree" (pp. 198–199). It is interesting that these qualities appear in many ways more cultural than biological. Eugenics, as Hollingworth understood it, would "ultimately reduce misery if the stupid, the criminal, and other mentally, physically, and morally deficient would refrain from reproduction" (p. 199).

Given these views on the differential worth of immigrant groups, the plea for the gifted to have many children takes on a rather disturbing meaning. If Hollingworth believed that children with early American ancestry were morally superior to their Southern European classmates, then negative eugenic policies would be differentially applied to those recent immigrants. Once again, Hollingworth was not promoting a biological meritocracy so much as a racial meritocracy, with clear ethnic and class overtones.

By 1929 Hollingworth was writing for the journal *Eugenics*, and there she cast the issue of giftedness in terms of human capital and its worth to

the state, suggesting policies for its increase: "If our state were scientifically Utopian," she explained,

> instead of romantically prejudiced against the teachings of biology and psy-
> chology, [the increase in gifted children in the population] might be accom-
> plished by paying to the parents of a child who tests ... above a set mini-
> mum in the qualities desired, a bonus in the probable value of such a child.
> (Hollingworth, 1929, pp. 6–7)

And that value had been determined: If the child were the offspring of a
scientist, its value would be $100,000.

It is true that we no longer accept the extreme assumptions of Wiggam,
Peters, Goddard, and Hollingworth as a rationale for a biological meritocracy. But it seems that we have not discarded their conception of an inherently unequal society based on biologically inherited merit as depicted
in a contemporary text such as Richard Herrnstein and Charles Murray's
The Bell Curve (1994).

Certainly it would be an error of both ethics and logic to assume that
since some in the history of education for the gifted supported eugenics,
current spokespersons also must be eugenicists. But to ignore the nondemo-
cratic, and in some cases racist, dimensions of that history is surely unwise.
In this time of a renewed interest in biological explanations for complex
human behavior, such a posture may be professionally irresponsible. Indeed, given today's continuing advances in the cloning of mammals, these
social attitudes need to be directly confronted as technology presents us
with the possibility of increasingly complex policy options (Kolata, 1997,
p. A1). The point here is that too few of today's educational professionals
preparing for work with gifted children realize this complexity in their
field's history.

CONCLUSION

The work of the authors we have just reviewed reveals them as a rather
tough-minded group. As they saw it, society had become too softhearted
toward its least worthy members and time and again they argued that a
just social order could exist only when each person could rise on his or her
own biological merit. But the achievement of a worthy and unequal social
order, as Wiggam, Peters, Goddard, and Hollingworth argued, had been
short-circuited by institutions that refused to see people as they *really were*.
People were different. They had differing inherited abilities and as a consequence they had differing social worth. In a society that offered equal
opportunity to all, people would become increasingly unequal. To stand

in the way of such inequality was to stand in the way of progress and science. In the case of these educational leaders, the science they chose was the putative science of eugenics.

Today, as we deepen our understanding of human genetics—a field that is not synonymous with eugenics—we also should consider carefully our theories concerning the nature of the good society, the qualities of the worthy citizen, and the attributes of the good life (Wexler, 1992, p. 211). As Ashley Montagu pointed out more than five decades ago, humankind, "it is very much to be feared, is not to be saved by bring treated like a lot of race horses or strains of dogs. Human beings must be treated like human beings first" (Montagu, 1942, p. 144). I take Montagu's point to be that when the issue is that of social justice, then ethics and science must be dialectically related. As this chapter suggests, educators like Wiggam, Peters, Goddard, and Hollingworth ignored such advice. We should not repeat that error. We need to take advantage of the opportunity to shape today's social policies. If Montagu is correct, such policies will serve as the ethical context for tomorrow's scientific insights and will prove to be of central importance to our students. In a sense, this work requests that we resist forces that would increase inequality in society by claiming that science somehow requires it. This is not a call to politicize our professional roles or to reject scientific data. It is simply a call to be aware that we are the inheritors of a professional past that includes a tradition of productive resistance. In the chapter that follows we will consider just such resistance to the popular Eugenics movement in the period prior to the Great Depression.

CHAPTER 6

Resisting American Eugenics

We cannot measure intelligence when we have never defined it, and we cannot speak of its hereditary basis after it has been indistinguishably fused with a thousand educational and environmental influences from the time of conception to the school age. The claim that Mr. Terman or anyone else is measuring hereditary intelligence has no more scientific foundation than a hundred fads, vitamins and glands, and amateur psychoanalysis and correspondence courses in will power, and it will pass with them into that limbo where phrenology and palmestry and characterology, and the other Babu sciences are to be found.
—Walter Lippmann, The New Republic, 1922

To this point in our analysis we have traced the impact of Eugenics on American education. From national congresses and conferences that drew leading intellectuals and academics to the strong words of support from presidents and the popular press, we have seen that eugenics was more than merely a movement at society's fringes. We have considered the numerous ways in which eugenics was popularized within the professional educational community. Whether in high school science, the undergraduate course of study, or professional programs for the preparation of future teachers, we have seen how eugenics made its mark. But readers may well find themselves more than a bit concerned here. After all, despite the extreme views and policies of many popularizers of eugenics, the movement still garnered the support of many educators and professional organizations. Did no one resist? That is, one may reasonably ask who else with national stature besides Ashley Montagu spoke out against this movement that viewed humankind and social policy as driven primarily by the insights from an extreme hereditarian interpretation of human development. These are legitimate concerns and what follows deals with those concerns directly.

This chapter identifies and details a series of arguments made against the basic assumptions of eugenics by members of the academy, the popular press, and the sciences. It reviews the work of individuals who resisted determinist eugenics. As with our previous analyses, all is not quite what it appears at first blush; as we shall see in the case of William Chandler

Bagley, resistance will turn out to be support. But the major point of this chapter will be that a fair rendering of the history of eugenics and its impact on American education does indeed reveal a well-articulated and substantive resistance to the movement and to its policy implications.

When we consider the relationship between racism and biology, we should not assume that genetics somehow makes individuals racist or that racism is impossible without the imprimatur of biological science. For surely that is not the case. Biology has what one might call "requirements," but not one of them mandates that one be a race thinker. Individuals and organizations with racial animus and determinist leanings did not need genetics in order to make their case. For example, as Ruth Elson has pointed out, it was quite possible for the geographies of the late 19th century to argue for a hierarchical scale of racial worth without mention of the biological sciences at all (Elson, 1964).

But by the 20th century a number of changes in genetics had combined to empower those who viewed programs of human breeding as a simple matter of controlling and/or combining separate hereditary characters from one generation to the next. These changes included August Weismann's rejection of the inheritance of acquired characters; Francis Galton's British coining of the term *eugenics*; and the rediscovery of Mendel's pioneering work on "hard" or particulate inheritance (Mayr, 1982, pp. 698–707).

While the Eugenics movement achieved a number of significant social policy successes, they were achieved in the face of an articulate resistance. It was a resistance that rejected eugenics from a variety of perspectives. By 1915, for example, many biologists rejected the eugenicists' simple Mendelian explanation for significant racial differences. Essentially these biologists concluded that the new genetic findings contradicted the eugenicists' view that all human qualities were based on single discrete factors.

Among those who rejected eugenics one finds Wesleyan University biologist Herbert William Conn, and Johns Hopkins biologist Herbert Spencer Jennings. Their work acknowledged the complexity of biological processes, which they reasoned made Mendelian eugenics problematic. Not only did environment play an important role in their views on biological development, but they also viewed social and cultural evolution as an important factor in human development. As Conn pointed out in the introduction to his *Social Heredity and Social Evolution: The Other Side of Eugenics* (1914):

> The purpose of this work is to show that the laws of the evolution of animals and plants apply to human evolution only up to a certain point, beyond which man has been under the influence of distinct laws of his own. . . . In doing this there will be given a sketch of the evolution of what we call civilization,

for such a sketch will show that social evolution has been controlled and guided by a new force which we will call *social hereditary*, a force which has had almost nothing to do with the evolution of the rest of the organic world, and one which acts practically independently of the laws which the eugenicists are disclosing to view. (pp. v–vi, emphasis in original)

A central assumption of those who resisted eugenics was that it could no longer stand on a nature *versus* nurture foundation. These two forces had to be related in a far more dialectical fashion. As Thomas Hunt Morgan and his colleagues (1915) were to show, even in the case of the fruit fly, heredity was dialectically related to environment.

The review of scientists, educators, and publicists that follows suggests that their resistance to eugenics was equally complex. While rejecting certain aspects of eugenics, they did not agree on all issues. And while they all held for the import of environment and hereditary in human development, all the writers considered did not reject eugenics. Indeed, as we shall see, Herbert Jennings allowed for eugenics programs only after social melioration had taken place; John Dewey never used the term, while he clearly rejected the determinism of the group IQ tests; William Chandler Bagley rejected a socially destructive determinism but embraced eugenics and race thinking; and Walter Lippmann rejected the competence of IQ tests to measure *hereditary* intelligence while accepting the usefulness of vocational testing.

In his excellent analysis of the nature–nurture controversy, Cravens (1978) describes the growing gap between early 20th century eugenicists' scientific understandings and progress in the field of genetics at that time. As these natural and social scientists learned of the complexity of genetics, their views on eugenics changed. Neutrality and passive support turned into outright rejection and leading scientists such as T. H. Morgan and Franz Boas rejected the eugenists' simple Mendelian explanations for complex human social and behavioral differences.

While surely not causal, links between economic ideology and biology can be made, and such links are most suggestive for those trying to understand the role and acceptance of eugenics in the early 20th century. Allen (1986) argues that if 19th-century laissez-faire capitalism needed notions of Darwinian survival, then 20th-century capitalism was well served by Galton's corporate eugenics. But once again, there were those who resisted.

Cravens (1978) traces this resistance to eugenics from the 1910s, in the work of Columbia University Nobel Laureate Thomas Hunt Morgan, to the capstone statement of 1947 by Theodosious Dobzhanshky and M. F. Ashley Montagu. The message they delivered was consistent across the decades. To the eugenicists' claim that nature was paramount in human development, they pointed out that development was a dialectical process; both nature and nurture were at play. They further argued that while humankind was indeed part of the natural order, it was nevertheless unique as the only species to undergo social as well as biological evolution. And it was this cultural evolution that set humankind apart. As Dobzhansky and Montagu (1947) pointed out, "instead of having [their] responses genetically fixed as in other animal species, [humankind] is a species that invents [its] own responses, and it is out of this unique ability to invent . . . that . . . cultures are born" (p. 500).

It was just such inventions that would trouble eugenicists. Concerned for social control as they were, they were interested in humankind's determination, not in its freedom. They were interested in social control and prediction, not in open-ended human inventions. Nevertheless, by this century's second decade the resistance was identifiable. Mainline eugenicists would be slow to accede to their critics' points, but they could not ignore them. Indeed, as criticism mounted, mainline eugenics was transformed into a seemingly less racist movement (Kevles, 1985, pp. 164–175).

As members of the academy, the immigrant community, and the media actively resisted popular eugenics in the 1920s, they pointed to the importance of *environment* in the heredity-environment controversy and to the above-mentioned dialectical nature of development (Cravens, 1978, pp. 224–265). Of the many psychological concepts and instruments that drew the attention of these critics, perhaps few were as quickly grasped by the general public as that of the newly created mental tests. The tests became a lightning rod for the debates about nature and nurture, the causes of crime, and the possibility of human racial differences.

Three foci fed a national anxiety about the intelligence of the American people and drew the attention of early mental testers. They included racial psychology, the relationship between low intelligence and crime, and the relationship between intelligence and social status. Cravens (1978) argues that it was around first of these, racial psychology, that the earliest and most heated debates about eugenics developed. As we saw in Chapter 2, when Carl Brigham (1923) published his analyses of the World War I Alpha and Beta test results, he used the work of the racist William Z. Ripley (1899) as the basis for his interpretations. Perhaps not surprisingly, Brigham concluded that America's ethnic diversity was a threat to national welfare and he cast his hereditarian prescriptions in ethnic and racial terms.

Black Americans, Brigham claimed, were racially inferior to their Nordic countrymen and an enlightened social policy must take heed of these findings. Even such seemingly disconfirming findings as the superior performance levels of northern blacks over those of their southern counterparts on the exams did not shake Brigham's hereditarian bias. He suggested that blacks who migrated north were genetically more intelligent and ambitious than their southern counterparts and this explained the differences in their test scores (Brigham, 1923). Even though African Americans (in the North at least) manifested these positive genetic qualities, Brigham did not recommend their social integration with America's Northern European immigrants. In fact, as Cravens reports, "Brigham solemnly concluded his book by calling for immigration restriction to preserve America's precious heritage of 'Nordic' germ plasm" (1978, p. 229). While this position was congenial for the members of the newly formed Galton Society, it did not sit well with a variety of others in the academy, public life, and the press. Motivated in different cases by insights drawn from science or social policy, these critics resisted the extreme hereditarianism of Brigham's interpretation.

From a contemporary perspective it is easy to see that this academic and ethnic resistance was not nearly as effective in constraining eugenics as were factors such as the economic collapse of the 1930s and the Second World War. Yet it is important for the reader to recognize that resistance existed. While we understand that eugenics influenced teacher training and biology textbooks in the interwar years, a mature historiography demands that we recognize both eugenics' detractors and its supporters. Among these many critics of mainline eugenics one can find the anthropologist Franz Boas; the educators John Dewey and William Chandler Bagley; the immigrant academic and civic leaders Abraham Myerson (professor of neurology at Tufts Medical College), Gustave Feingold, and Maurice B. Hexter (of the Federated Jewish Charities of Boston); and the *New Republic* political journalist and social critic Walter Lippmann. In order to develop a better sense of the complexity of the history of eugenics and American education, we will review the nature of the arguments made against eugenics by Jennings, Dewey, Bagley, and Lippmann.

H. S. JENNINGS: NATURE AND NURTURE IN THE BIOLOGICAL SCIENCES

The work of H. S. Jennings exemplifies resistance to eugenics from within the scientific community. Unlike Bagley and Dewey, whose focus was cast in terms of social policy or pedagogy, Jennings was a professional biologist. During the period between the world wars, he and a group of like-minded colleagues (including Lancelot Hogben, J. B. S. Haldane, and Julian Huxley) worked "to expose the fallacies, to disencumber the vocabulary, to cleanse the use of their science" (Kevles, 1985, p. 128). Scientists who were aware of the rapid changes taking place in biology during the century's first two decades used these understandings to join in the ongoing debate about the role of nature and nurture in human development. One point of contention was the notion that for every human trait there was a single, discrete, nonblending factor or character. Judging this popular interpretation of Mendelian single factor–single trait correspondence to be inadequate and misleading, Jennings took to the pages of the popular media and to the halls of Congress to express his resistance.

In early 1924 Congress was debating the immigration bill that would become the restrictive Johnson-Reed act. The nativist Henry H. Laughlin was serving as a scientific consultant to the committee and his extreme views on genetics and race appeared to have deeply offended Jennings's sense of probity. In Jennings's view, Laughlin's testimonials to Nordic supremacy had gone far beyond the limits of scientific evidence. John N. Vaile's testimony before the committee on April 1924 is an example of the sort of celebratory presentation that Laughlin valued and Jennings rejected. After first denying the claim that the Nordic race was the best, Vaile concluded that America was nevertheless a Nordic country and he was determined that it remain so. "Let me emphasize," he explained to the committee, "that the 'restrictionists' of Congress do not claim that the 'Nordic' race . . . is the best race in the world. [But that race] made this country."

> Oh, yes; the others helped. But that is the full statement of the case. They came to this country because it was already made as an Anglo-Saxon commonwealth. They added to it, they often enriched it, but they did not make it, and they have not yet greatly changed it. . . . It suits us. And what we assert is that we are not going to surrender it to somebody else or allow other people, no matter what their merits, to make it something different. If there is any changing to be done, we will do it ourselves. (Ludmerer, 1972, pp. 109–110)

When Jennings was at last invited to address the committee, he was given but a few minutes in an afternoon crowded with other witnesses and was then asked to present his remarks in written form. Even scheduling could be used as a control device. As Ludmerer (1972) notes, "such was the treatment given the one man whom even Laughlin was later to deem worthy of a reply" (pp. 109–110).

Jennings would continue to argue for the complementary role of nature and nurture in development. The examples he cited, which were striking in 1930, give one pause even to this day. They included embryonic cells that could become either skin or spinal cord in response to varying environmental influences; paramecia whose appearance was contingent on environment; fruit flies whose genetic potentialities were dependent on humidity levels for their expression; and corn and primroses whose colors were contingent on environmental changes (Jennings, 1930, chap. 5).

Jennings, author of *The Biological Basis of Human Nature* (1930), "knew from biology itself that, from the fetal stage onward, nurture acted upon nature to shape the organism. The chemical and physical environment could affect germ cells—sperm and ova—prior to fertilization" (Kevles, 1985, pp. 142–143). Using drawings depicting those remarkable differences, Jennings (1930) described an experiment in which the water-living salamander, axolotl, was transformed into the land salamander, amblystoma. The transformation was effected through a change in the environment of the axolotl, through a change in its diet. Jennings described the procedure as follows:

> As we saw, if the young [water-living] axolotl is fed on thyroid, it undergoes a tremendous transformation, comparable to that which changes a tadpole into a frog. It loses its gills; its body form alters in every detail, so that it is no longer adapted for swimming. It crawls out on the land and becomes the land salamander known as Amblystoma. . . . Its characteristics have become completely changed. On land it lives for the rest of its life, going to the water only to lay its eggs. (p. 124)

The implications for questions of nature and nurture for mankind were obvious to Jennings (1930). His recommendations for improving the human diet and for the positive influences of vitamins A, D, C, and E on developing human fetuses, neonates, children, and adults were drawn directly from his insights as to the importance of environmental factors in development.

Recalling Davenport's earlier reference to the determinism of characteristics, we can now see where Jennings's response was directed. "In organisms as we find them in nature," he rhetorically asked,

> are the characteristics of the individuals altered by the external conditions under which they live, the physical and the social conditions that affect them? May diverse characteristics result from diverse outer conditions? In other words, are the products of the interaction of the genes and cytoplasm different under different external conditions? (Jennings, 1930, p. 127)

To each of these queries he answered an unqualified yes. Heredity and environment do interact. The mainline eugenicists were wrong. Social evils were not simply a matter of bad genes and their elimination. And Jennings cried "nonsense" to the "eugenic claim that environmental improvement—public health measures, social services, better wages and working conditions—fostered the survival of the 'unfit'" (Kevles, 1985, p. 143).

Having presented insights from the changing landscape of biological science, Jennings (1930) then dealt with issues that were important to Dewey and other educators of the period. Whether in biology or mental testing, he pointed out, the issue is one of careful analysis of the environment for its influence on both phenotype and test scores. Jennings demanded that

> measures of public health must be carried out, overwork and bad conditions of living done away with, faults in diet, both quantitative and qualitative, corrected; economic ills conquered, [and] grinding poverty abolished. When these things are done, when the human plant is given conditions under which it can unfold its capabilities without stunting, poisoning and mutilation by the environment, then it will be possible to discover what ills are due primarily to defective genes. (p. 250)

It was just this question of the relationship between biology and social policy that Dewey would consider as he addressed a national convention of black Americans at the end of this century's first decade.

JOHN DEWEY: THE INDIVIDUAL AND RESISTANCE TO CLASSIFICATION

John Dewey was America's premier progressive educator during the first half of the 20th century and he took positions on the majority of the significant social questions of his day. Yet a search of the corpus of his work reveals no direct reference to eugenics. While many of his Teachers College colleagues supported eugenics, his lack of direct confrontation with the movement does not suggest his tacit acceptance of its goals or purposes. If the eugenics movement hoped for a biologically stratified society of differential rewards, Dewey did not. If eugenicists believed that mental tests could and should be used for classification as opposed to diagnostic purposes, Dewey did not. If the eugenicists distrusted democracy and longed for a biologically determined intellectual aristocracy, Dewey did not. And lastly, if many among the movement's followers felt that humankind could be classified into discrete races of varying worth, Dewey did not. He spoke out against the issue of racial differentiation and used his broad understanding of science to buttress that position.

When addressing the National Negro Conference in 1909, for example, he placed his rejection of racism in the context of work he had recently published on social policy and biological science regarding the discredited theory of acquired characteristics (Dewey, 1909). Displaying an understanding of changes under way in biology, he attacked the issue of racism directly. "It was for a long time the assumption," he explained, "that acquired characteristics of heredity, in other words the capacities which the individual acquired through his home life and training, modified the stock that was handed down" (quoted in Boydston, 1977, p. 156). But "the whole tendency of biological science at the present time," he continued, "is to make it reasonably certain that characteristics which the individual acquired are not transmissible" (p. 156). While some might find the fact that one cannot transmit one's personal achievements to one's children a cause for disappointment, Dewey counseled against despair. He assured his listeners that these findings were "very encouraging" (p. 156). Consistent with his concern for individuality rather than individualism, he explained that "so far as individuals are concerned . . . [it means] that they have a full, fair and free social opportunity."

> Each generation biologically commences over again very much on the level of the individuals of the past generation, or a few generations gone by. In other words, there is no "inferior race," and the members of a race so-called should have the same opportunities of social environment and personality as those of a more favored race. (p. 157)

Dewey was direct in his policy prescriptions. He recommended that society make opportunities available to all in order that each might realize his or her potential regardless of ethnicity.

Here we see Dewey's progressive dream of an equitable society in which all members would be able to maximize their potential, free of unreasonable constraints. Observing that individuals in all races varied and that no race had a range of individuals that exceeded any other, Dewey concluded that it was in the self-interest of science and society to demand equitable treatment for African Americans. A full decade and a half before Brigham would type Americans by intellect and ethnicity, Dewey had prepared his rebuttal:

> All points of skill are represented in every race and a society that does not furnish the environment and education and the opportunity of all kinds which will bring out and make effective the superior ability wherever it is born, is not merely doing an injustice to that particular race and to those particular individuals, but it is doing an injustice to itself for it is depriving itself of just that much of social capital. (quoted in Boydston, 1977, p. 157)

Dewey's position on the importance of biology for social policy is clear; biology presents each generation with a new array of potentiality. To view this set of possibilities in racial terms is not only to limit the future of those erroneously judged inferior but to deny society needed social competence. It is not hard to read between the lines and see how biology, individuality, and merit were joined together in Dewey's rejection of this destructive racial type-casting for the creation of a democratic polity.

Yet it was just these categories that were combined by later reform eugenicists to bolster their recommended programs of racially neutral human breeding. For those later reformers, the measurement of intellectual merit by intelligence tests, the issue of individuality, and the role of biology in human development were central to proposals for programs of positive and negative eugenics. Although Dewey may never have written specifically of eugenics, he seems to have recognized that there were some who would use intelligence tests for inappropriate social policy purposes. In this regard he was more than willing to speak out in critique. Such a public critique took place in December 1922 in the pages of the political journal *The New Republic*. Having rejected racial aristocracies, he now went on to reject intellectual aristocracies as well.

In many ways, Dewey's critique of mental tests was that they viewed their subjects in broad categories that denied individuality. Indeed, when Dewey penned "Mediocrity and Individuality" in 1922 this was exactly the issue he raised. He rejected a process of classification that submerged the individual into "average aggregates" and warned that such classifications may "postpone the day of a reform of education which will get us away from inferior, mean and superior mediocrities so as to deal with individualized mind and character" (p. 35). As with his colleagues in the biological sciences, Dewey recognized that education and social policy needed proper consideration of individual differences. While there is much to be gained by viewing the subtlety in Dewey's response in the context of transformations in biological theory, he was also quite aware of the politically conservative social meanings that could be erroneously be drawn from the intelligence test data.

An example of such an erroneous interpretation of intelligence tests can be found in Colgate University President George B. Cutten's inaugural remarks, which were reprinted in *School and Society* in 1922. Cutten argued that America could not sustain a democratic form of government unless intelligence tests were used to identify the "intellectual aristocracy" from which the nation's rulers must be selected He even went so far as to argue that democracy was "out of the question" (p. 479) and that America needed a society of differing castes. Typical of those of the period who would "sing the praise[s] of mental tests as capable of evaluating a heterogeneous population in scientific and systematic fashion" (Cravens, 1978, p. 225), he became the target of Dewey's displeasure on the pages of the *New Republic*. "Mr. Cutten," Dewey noted, "begins his presidential career with a view of the social stratification which is to be the ultimate outcome of an educational classification by means of mental testing."

> We are to arrive at a caste system like that of India, "but on a just and ratio-
> nal basis." For "when the tests of vocational guidance are completed and de-
> veloped, each boy and girl in school will be assigned to the vocation for which
> he is fitted." There will be no difficulty in filling the ranks of unskilled labor
> . . . for Mr. Cutten implicitly believes the yarn that the army tests have shown
> that the "average mentality" of the population is slightly over thirteen years.
> (Dewey, 1922, p. 35)

"Considering only the energy and unspoiled curiosity of the average thir-
teen year old in comparison with the dulled observation and blunted vigor
of the average adult," Dewey concluded, "one might hope that this statement were true" (p. 35).

Dewey is well known for his rejection of education for specific vocational
preparation and he noted that "an I.Q. as at presently determined is at most
an indication of certain abilities. Its practical value lies in the stimulus its gives
to more intimate and intense inquiry into individualized abilities and disabilities" (Dewey, 1922, p. 35). Here we need to recognize that he was not
against mental testing, in principle. He was, however, against mental testing that merely took individuals and classified them as members of a larger
set. He was against testing that disregarded the individual or saw intelligence as pessimistically fixed. For such testing and such thinking affords
"striking evidence of the habit of ignoring specific individualities, of thinking
in terms of fixed classes, intellectual and social" (p. 35). Opposed to the way
in which the nature-nurture argument had been framed, his well-practiced
Hegelianism kept him from accepting such dichotomous propositions.

Dewey was always searching for a transformation of dualities; it is not
nature versus nurture, we seem to hear him say, but rather nature *and*
nurture that explains human progress. Is intelligence fixed? Is nature more
important than nurture? Do innate abilities set limits on performance?
These are serious questions for the educator and the policymaker. Cutten
was more than willing to answer in the affirmative; not so Dewey. "No
matter how much innate qualities may set limits," he explained, "they are
not active forces."

> Experience, that is to say education, is the mother of wisdom. And we shall
> never have any light upon what are the limits to intelligence set by innate
> qualities till we have immensely modified our scheme of getting and giving
> experience, of education. Barring complete imbecility, it is safe to say that the
> most limited member of the populace has potentialities which do not now
> reveal themselves and which will not reveal themselves till we convert edu-
> cation by and for mediocrity into an education by and for individuality.
> (Dewey, December 1922, p. 37)

These comments could have just as easily have been made by the biologist Jennings and in many ways they are similar to the position taken by Dewey's colleague at Teachers College, William Chandler Bagley. Yet Bagley's comments on testing, the nature–nurture debate, and race suggest a different type of criticism than those considered so far. For William Chandler Bagley, it will turn out, was a rather ambivalent critic.

WILLIAM CHANDLER BAGLEY: THE AMBIVALENT CRITIC

Bagley received his doctorate from Cornell University after completing a correlational study of human intellectual and physical characteristics. He was to spend virtually his entire career in the field of education and after 1917 he maintained his tenure at Columbia University's Teachers College. Attempts to categorize Bagley in liberal or conservative terms run the risk of oversimplifying the man. In his views of curriculum content one might well call him a conservative; his curricular essentialism, which valued traditional content, placed him in conflict with educational theorists who wanted the curriculum to have relevance to students' lives or to have immediate vocational application. While Bagley might not have approved of the process used by current educational leaders to identify a common core of Western values and traditions for all schoolchildren, he would undoubtedly approve of the overall concept.

In the case of the nature–nurture debate however, insofar as a liberal interpretation is seen as favoring the influence of environment, Bagley was a liberal. His interest in the controversy predates the public interest in what Cravens (1978) has called "racial psychology" and it suggests that Bagley did not easily come to his environmentalist conclusions. Bagley "shifted on the nature–nurture issue at least twice."

> In the early 1900s [Bagley] believed that a good education could overcome any inherited deficiencies. He submitted an article containing that thesis to *Popular Science Monthly* in 1907. But in the fall of 1908 he asked the publisher, J. McKeen Cattell, not to publish his article because he had changed his mind; "the studies of Frederick Woods and the conclusions of such men as [E. L.] Thorndike and [Karl] Pearson have lead me to very radically . . . modify the views I expressed in the paper." Woods, Thorndike and Pearson had argued with seemingly impressive statistical proof that heredity prevailed over environment in intelligence. In the 1910s, however, Bagley [had changed his mind again and he] became more and more convinced that the functional psychologists, who argued that innate nature adjusted to cultural environment, were closer to the truth than the hereditarians. (Cravens, 1978, p. 230)

As Bagley was taking issue with the extreme hereditarian view on the importance of nature in human development, popular sentiment was being shaped by the Army classification examinations, which received wide currency by 1921. Their findings were being interpreted in both racial and hereditarian terms. By the middle of the decade the pages of *School and Society* carried articles reflecting this hereditarian view. One article argued that the Army tests required a stratified social order and a society differentiated by measures of intelligence. In such a perfectly rationalized society, William Tait (1925) reasoned, there would be many who would "only [be] fit to be hewers of wood, but they should be expert hewers."

> Those who are not fit for higher education should be fully trained in the line for which they may be specially fitted. They should be told what to do, how to do it, and when to do it. They should be trained but not educated. . . . If democracy is to come to its own by getting the best out of each, then it must do so by the scientific process of selection and elimination, thus creating an intellectual elite. (p. 37)

Bagley saw the ideas of men such as Tait as a threat to democracy. In *Determinism in Education* (1925), he excoriated them with eloquence and statistics and questioned the assumption that the Army tests were "trustworthy measures of native intelligence" (p. 115).

While some in the 1920s would criticize eugenics for its racist associations or inappropriate scientific warrants, Bagley (1922) argued that it was determinism that directly threatened both democracy and social cohesion. These concerns, and his belief in the powers of environmental reform, drove his analysis. "The current teachings of educational determinism," he warned, "are dangerous because they proceed with a dogmatic disregard for the possibilities of insuring progress through environmental agencies. This disregard is so studied, so pointed, as to brand the determinist as thoroughly prejudiced" (p. 376). It was the insurance of progress through environmental reform that became a significant point of difference between Bagley and men such as Brigham. Further, Bagley's use of the term *prejudiced* has a slightly different meaning from today's commonsense understanding of the term. Throughout *Determinism and Education* (1925), Bagley linked prejudice with belief in the hereditarian hypothesis on human intelligence, not necessarily with an a priori belief in racial inequality. It is this latter meaning, that of accepting differences in intelligence by race, that we would today associate with the term. Yet it is reasonably clear from Bagley's own words that while he resisted determinism, he did not take the position of a racial egalitarian.

Bagley's self-professed position was that of the "rational equalitarian." The rational equalitarian position was composed of two racial assumptions

and one social prescription. The rational equalitarian accepted race differences between whites and blacks, held as problematic evidence supporting
differences between white "strains," and supported education as a means
of uplift for all groups. When it came to intellectual differences between races,
Bagley agreed with C. C. Brigham's (1923) data but not his extreme policies.
As he noted, his alternative to Brigham's program did "not quarrel with facts;
hence it does not deny racial differences in intelligence levels."

> It recognizes a fair degree of probability that the Negro race will never pro-
> duce so large a proportion of highly gifted persons as the white races. It rec-
> ognizes that certain of the white strains may be more prolific in talent and
> genius than certain others; but it also holds that, in the present state of knowl-
> edge, invidious distinctions cannot safely be drawn among Nordics, Alpines,
> and Mediterraneans in this regard. (Bagley, 1925, p. 129)

Having thus allowed for innate differences between the white and black
races but not within divisions in the white race, Bagley (1925) went on to
argue that the "level of effective intelligence in any group of whatever race
can be substantially raised through education" (p. 129). Schooling, he instructed his readers, might never equalize America's racial diversity but it
could facilitate the achievement of all groups.

It is important to underscore Bagley's points here as they are little told
by other analysts of his work. Bagley (1925) saw schooling as critical if the
nation was to avoid civil strife. To accept the hereditarian program and its
social policy implications, he warned, was to accept the inevitability of
violent social upheaval.

> The hereditarian's solution to the problem is intolerant of the facts that do
> not support it: it is openly inhumane and blatantly anti-democratic; and to
> make it work would involve an upheaval beside which the late war would
> look like an afternoon tea. (p. 131)

A careful reading of Bagley's *Determinism in Education* (1925) today is
both informative and provocative. In 1925 Bagley offered a rousing critique
of the seemingly fatalistic implications of Brigham's (1923) work. It was a
critique driven by a concern for social stasis that used statistical analyses
to make its points. Bagley was surely one of education's most careful critics of Brigham's interpretations of the Army mental tests. But while interested in uncovering the limitations of the hereditarian view of human intelligence, he was motivated neither by a sense of racial equality nor by a
rejection of eugenics. In what we may find a surprising set of recommendations, he concluded a criticism of pro-Nordic propaganda with suggestions at a midpoint between the mainline and the reform eugenicist.

> The rational equalitarian proposes: 1) a vast extension of educational facili-
> ties and a far-reaching refinement of educational materials and methods; and
> 2) among other objectives the direction of educational agencies toward a) the
> establishment of race-purity in all major races, and b) a voluntary acceptance
> of eugenics practices to the end, that in all races, the reproduction of less
> worthy stock may be reduced. (Bagley, 1925, p. 130)

These recommendations demand our attention today because they suggest
that Bagley's quarrel was with Brigham's determinism and not with his
view of possible race differences. They indicate that while Bagley was an
antideterminist he was nevertheless a race thinker.

Recalling Kevles' (1985) distinctions between the mainline and the reform versions of eugenics may be of help in understanding the proposals of
the rational equalitarian. Mainline eugenicists recommended differential
breeding programs in terms of race. Those racial types they judged unfit
should be constrained from breeding. Reform eugenicists, on the other hand,
recommended differential breeding regardless of race. They would encourage the "best" to breed with the "best." Interestingly enough, Bagley's rational equalitarian program was halfway between the policies of these two
groups. That is, he supported a set of parallel mainline eugenics programs
in which each race would breed only from its best and never with other races.
The rational equalitarian position supported eugenics and it is here that
education has its part to play.

The rational equalitarian, Bagley (1925) explained, "holds that coer-
cion can never accomplish the ends that eugenics seeks but that appropriate education may lead to the desired practices" (p. 130). Education in this
view serves as a remarkable palliative. It can achieve the eugenicists' joint
ends of keeping the races genetically separate while avoiding measures that
would "quickly entail an interracial war" (p. 129). Such warfare would be
avoided by the application of rational equalitarian policies, which propose
that "diverse racial stocks can learn to live together and to work together
without necessitating a blend of blood, and that undesirable blends of blood
can be prevented through education" (p. 130).

Bagley rejected Brigham's conclusions in *A Study of American Intelligence*
(1923). He countered that score-differentials between early and recent immigrants and northern and southern blacks more reasonably supported an
environmentalist position on human improvement. A consideration of the
environment was critical if one were to accept Bagley's primary position. It
was a position that allowed for both nature and nurture in human development while accepting one primary difference—that of race.

In Bagley's prescriptions for a just society, races would remain separate genetically but would work together socially. Rational equalitarian-
ism, he instructed his readers,

differs from the program of the hereditarian in being more nearly consistent with the observed facts, in being in harmony with the ideals of humanity and democracy that have been winnowed and refined through the ages, and above all in being workable. (Bagley, 1925, p. 131)

Whether *workable* would be a term used by those who were to remain racially separate and disenfranchised in the 1930s is not for this study to determine, but the consequences of Bagley's analyses are a legitimate topic for consideration.

Bagley's contribution to recasting the debate of nature versus nurture into one of nature and nurture is an important one. Many historians argue that his careful analysis of the Brigham data was a factor leading to the publication of the National Society for the Study of Education (NSSE) yearbook, *Nature and Nurture* (Whipple, 1928). Interestingly enough, Bagley's resolution was to give impetus to a new research agenda concerned with the varying and separate influence of nature and nurture in human development. These studies, primarily of identical twins, would lead to yet new debates, and they have now developed a history of their own (Fancher, 1985; Kamin, 1974; Selden, 1987).

WALTER LIPPMANN AND THE MEASUREMENT OF HEREDITARY INTELLIGENCE

The issue of the influence of heredity on human performance and psychologists' ability to measure that influence in an objective fashion was an issue of public discussion in the early 1920s. In October and November 1922 for example, the *New Republic* carried a series of articles by the liberal political journalist Walter Lippmann. With wit and insight, Lippmann attacked what he judged the false assumptions and potential abuses of mental tests. He argued that mainline eugenicists disregarded the findings of both biologists and social critics as to the importance and legitimacy of environment in physical, social, and intellectual development.

Lippmann's focus was also on the Alpha and Beta tests and specifically on Lewis M. Terman's Stanford revision of the Binet test. In a fashion similar to that of Jennings, he argued that the development of intelligence (even allowing for the testers' problematic interpretation of the term) was surely the consequence of the interplay of nature and nurture. He also argued that the mental testers' descriptive measures were being used for political purposes by hereditarian extremists. Lippmann pointed out that Lathrop Stoddard, racist author of *The Rising Tide of Color Against White World-Supremacy* (1920), had repeated the popular nostrum that the average mental age of Americans was only about 13 in order to increase the national anxiety about America's intellectual capacities. With barbed sarcasm, Lippmann responded that "the average adult intelligence cannot be less than the average adult intelligence" and that to say this was "as silly as [to say] that the average mile was three-quarters of a mile long. For the statement that the average mental age of Americans is only about fourteen is not inaccurate. It is not incorrect. It is nonsense" (Lippmann, 1922b, p. 213).

His telling critique also included technical analyses of the reliability of the intelligence tests, the procedures for norming the Binet, and the lack of definition of the term *intelligence* itself. These well-articulated criticisms are worth a contemporary reading as they cut to the heart of issues that today are almost lost beneath the sophisticated statistical technology that has developed in the intervening years.

Lippmann's most powerful criticisms were not of the technology of testing but of the test constructors' major assumptions. He argued (1922d) that the intelligence tests of his day rested on three major assumptions: (1) that intelligence was overwhelmingly hereditary and unchangeable; (2) that the tests measured hereditary intelligence; and (3) that education was essentially impotent in the face of such determinist truths (p. 277). With considerable elegance, Lippmann separated the first two of these issues. As to the first point, he never proposed that intelligence was not inherited. His focus was on the testers' assumptions about the object of their instruments. "It is not necessary for our purpose to come to any conclusion as to the inheritance of capacity."

> We are concerned only with the claim of the intelligence tester that he reveals and measures hereditary intelligence. These are quite separate propositions, but they are constantly confused by the testers. (p. 330)

As he saw it, part of the confusion came from the disregard that the testers and Terman in particular showed for early development. He chided that observing a child at age 4 and then assuming that intelligence tests could make a determination of innate capacity simply disregarded the impact of environment on IQ. "The whole drama of childhood," he correctly argued, "where the habits of intelligence are formed, is concealed in the mental tests" (Lippmann, 1922a, p. 9). This denial of development was a critical error on the part of the test constructors themselves. It was made in the very way in which Terman, for example, approached the issue of innate intelligence. "He cannot simply lump together the net result of natural endowment and infantile education," Lippmann (1922d) complained, "and [then] ascribe it to the germplasm" (p. 330). As Lippmann understood the issue, the test results reflected the interplay of nature and nurture; much to his distress the testers appeared insensitive to that insight. To make his point, he recounted a story in which Terman was alleged to have tested "twenty children in an orphanage and found only three who were fully normal. . . . Think of it," Lippmann noted with false surprise, "[Terman] first discovers what a 'normal' mental development is by testing children who have grown up in an adult environment of parents, aunts, and uncles."

> He then applies this footrule to children who are growing up in the abnormal environment of an institution and finds that they are not normal. He then puts the blame on the germplasm of the orphans. (p. 330)

In Lippmann's eyes, such misinterpretations were the consequence of the testers' unconscious will to believe, rather than to know. If we keep in mind that the above stories were told not in order to reject the hereditary nature of intelligence but rather to moderate the excessive claims of the testers, we can easily see how Lippmann (1922a) was able to conclude that "the claim that we have learned how to measure hereditary intelligence has no scientific foundation."

> We cannot measure intelligence when we have never defined it, and we cannot speak of its hereditary basis after it has been indistinguishably fused with a thousand educational and environmental influences from the time of conception to the school age. The claim that Mr. Terman or anyone else is measuring hereditary intelligence has no more scientific foundation than a hundred fads, vitamins and glands, and amateur psychoanalysis and correspondence courses in will power, and it will pass with them into that limbo where phrenology and palmestry and characterology, and the other Babu sciences are to be found. (p. 10)

We need to be careful here not to interpret Lippmann as some sort of psychometric nihilist; he was not categorically against testing. On the contrary, he strongly supported the vocational-placement uses of tests. As he suggested (1922d), not without some whimsy, "instead . . . of trying to find a test that will with equal success discover artillery officers, Methodist ministers and branch managers for the rubber business,"

> the psychologists would far better work out examinations for [these vocations]. On that line they may make a serious contribution to a civilization which is constantly searching for more successful ways of classifying people for specialized jobs. (p. 10)

The issue for Walter Lippmann in the early 1920s was that of creating a rational society in which tests could assist in vocational placement, while avoiding the trap of both idealizing and legitimating a biologically determined intellectual aristocracy. In many ways Lippmann's brilliant rejection of mental tests as a valid measure of hereditary intelligence was in keeping with Dewey's rejection of racial differences in intelligence. It was surely consistent with Jennings's demand that environment's critical role in development be considered, and it was equally consistent with Bagley's rejection of determinism.

CONCLUSION

Our analysis of the work of these resisters to eugenics reveals at least four somewhat contradictory findings. Initially we can see that each critic replaced the eugenicist's biological determinism with a more dialectical nature-nurture model and that in all but Bagley's case, biological interpretations of race were rejected for policy development. Interestingly enough, one may also conclude that these critics unwittingly planted the seeds of future debates about the role of heredity and merit in society. This foray into the history of the resistance to eugenics concludes with an observation regarding the reasons for its decline as well as with a question about its legacy for today's educators.

It was undoubtedly the public nature of the criticisms of Dewey, Jennings, and Lippmann that helped to turn public opinion against eugenics. As Cravens (1978) points out, "the decline of the eugenics movement's reputation among educated middle-class Americans owed far more to the public criticisms of eugenics made by recognized scientists after the early 1920s [than to information gained in academic settings]."

> Those who did not hear of the new ideas, or saw no relationship between them and eugenics, could nevertheless follow a drama in their daily newspapers and in popular magazines: the withdrawal of geneticists' support for eugenics and scientific racism. This was devastating for eugenics and scientific racism for their ultimate sanction lay in science; divested of that legitimacy of science, both were now perceived as elitist political ideologies. (p. 174)

There is a serious caveat, however, to this story's seemingly progressive ending in which truth triumphs over ignorance. As we have seen in prior chapters of this book, despite the rejection of eugenics by the scientific and academic communities in the late 1920s, the ideology of eugenics continued to be favorably presented in biology texts for high school students for the next two decades. These are seemingly difficult positions to reconcile. Perhaps the answer is to be found in the transformation eugenics underwent in the 1930s (Kevles, 1985, pp. 164–175) and in the legacy that remained from the resolution of the nature–nurture debate.

As historians of the movement are now coming to understand, eugenics came in two varieties. Kevles argues that the first or mainline eugenics had lost its scientific legitimacy after the criticisms of the 1920s. This form of racist eugenics was not only judged immoral, it was judged to have no scientific warrant. The second variety or reform eugenics was stripped of its racial overtones and appeared as a benign source of "nature" to the newly interactive vision of the nature–nurture debate. It was this latter eugenics that continued to gain acceptance and, some might argue, support in the post-1920s period. I believe the reason for this support has little to do with race thinking and much to do with the role of schools in sorting and selecting students. That is to say, reform eugenics continued to legitimate the vocational functions of the school in a period when the Social Efficiency Movement in curriculum planning reigned supreme. As Kliebard so eloquently argues, social efficiency was one of the major traditions in the historical struggle in the development of the American school curriculum (Kliebard, 1986). Unlike Dewey's commitment to social transformation, or Hall's concern for child development, social efficiency educators valued social organization over the individual. It was a movement with a strong process-product orientation toward research and it had powerful vocational interests. Within such a research program and in light of such instrumental interests, the variables of nature and nurture came to be seen as easily disaggregated. Determinations allegedly could be made of the relative contribution to human performance of these variables with outcomes presented in the seemingly neutral language of statistical comparisons. Decisions, on apparently nonideological grounds, then could be made as to the appropriate destination of the children in the nation's schools. In fact, as we saw in Chapter 4, this appears to be what happened in the case of the biology textbooks of the period. The texts considered eugenics, legitimated its scientific standing, offered support to programs of differential breeding, and recommended that vocational goals be informed if not directed by objective tests of inherited intelligence.

These were the sorts of proposals that Dewey had vociferously rejected. But the role that eugenics took in these texts is just the one that Colgate's Cutten (1922) had demanded. That is, the Cutten view remained a source of influence on both textbooks and classrooms in the period between the world wars, despite the protestations of Dewey, Bagley, Lippmann, and others.

It would be an error, however, to conclude with a pessimistic view of eugenics' apparent success. The story of the period is one of debate within the biological sciences and debate in the area of curriculum and policy. Competing views have been a tradition in curriculum studies and such debates require antagonists; they require proponents as well as resisters.

Traditions for resistance are part of our professional past. It is only for us to make them live in the present and the future. The point is not to be contentious for the sake of contentiousness. That is not what informed the work of Dewey, Bagley, Jennings, and Lippmann. They sought to anneal public policy debates with questions relating to empirical reality and social vision. They applied critical analysis and compassion to the central issues of their day. It is a tradition worthy of our continuing support.

Today, as in the early 20th century, the question we confront is that of linking complex human behavior and genetic markers. We are no longer so naive as to believe that simple Mendelian characteristics drive complex behavior and today scientists, unlike the uninformed eugenicists of the past, apply sophisticated statistical and molecular analyses to the task. Perhaps the day will come when complex social behavior is understood in terms of its markers. But given the history discussed in the previous five chapters, we have reason to be cautious. To that end, the following chapter offers critical analyses of a series of studies that propose to identify links between markers and complex behavior. The studies are taken seriously and some are found unconvincing. Yet the chapter neither rejects science nor denies the insights of biology. It continues rather in the tradition of Dewey and Lippmann, and applies thoughtful caution to the studies themselves. In this case, it is a caution that takes the form of resistance.

CHAPTER 7

Human Behavior and Biological Markers: A Cautionary Tale

> [*Research*] *directed towards seeking the origins of violence in US society in terms of the genotypes of blacks and poor inner-city whites, the problem of "temperament" in toddlers and the deficiencies in serotonin-reuptake mechanisms in incarcerated criminals, is clearly going to keep a generation of psychologists, neuropharmacologists and behavioural geneticists in research funds for a good few years to come. But as an approach to diminishing the violence of city streets it would seem unlikely to achieve as significant an impact as would measures to reduce the estimated 280 million handguns in personal possession in the United States.*
> —Stephen Rose, "The Rise of Neurogenetic Determinism," Nature, 1995

While the eugenics movement was surely moribund by the end of the Second World War, the issues that concerned its early 20th century supporters continue to vex the public as it moves toward the millennium. For example, attempts to resolve the nature–nurture debate and the desire to find biological substrates that might explain complex human behavior continue to this day as they demand a role in the development of public policy (Herrnstein & Murray, 1994). As noted earlier, the desire to clothe Plato's hereditarian metaphors of persons of silver, gold, and iron with scientific explanations has maintained a continuing place in American popular consciousness for nearly a century. Hereditarian social attitudes, as Haller (1963) points out, often serve as a distorting lens through which data on human development must pass. I want to be careful in making this point. I do not mean to suggest that where legitimate genetic evidence is available, as in the case of Tay-Sachs disease among others, one should disregard it. Rather, I want to point out that when issues such as class, gender, or race are at stake, hereditarian attitudes have the potential to distort legitimate scientific evidence and they can have disastrous social consequences. This of course was the case with the American Eugenics movement and Mendelian genetics early in this century. Nevertheless, this tension between social attitudes and scientific data presents the reader with the need to move carefully between the Scylla of a naive acceptance of biological determinism ("scientists have found markers for certain human medical conditions, so all of our behavior must be deter-mined by our genes") and the Charybdis of a mindless rejection of scientific evidence ("humankind is unique as a species; biological explanations of human behavior are irrelevant and 'politically incorrect'"). Having warned of the inappropriateness of such responses, I will in this chapter critically analyze a series of studies that link complex human behavior using chro-mosomal, DNA, and statistical analyses, in order to distinguish between re-search findings that can be appropriately used in developing social policy and those that cannot.

The research includes pedigree studies of allegedly feebleminded women, chromosomal studies of Trisomy-21 and XYY disjunctions, family and twin studies of antisocial behavior and sports activities, animal studies of the re-action to stress, and DNA marker studies of novelty-seeking and sexual orien-tation. As we shall see, in cases where the behavior and the marker are clearly and unambiguously defined, causal links may be logically inferred. However, in studies where phenotype and genotype are ambiguous, explanatory links between behavior and marker will be far more difficult to validate.

Humans are biological organisms and the following analyses are not presented as a rejection of attempts to explain various human traits in genetic terms. Indeed, our very presence as active organisms is the expres-sion of the dialectic of our biological inheritance and our life experiences. I do not reject behavior genetics out of hand. I would rather repeat a caveat made by Allen and Futterman (1995) regarding the wonderfully complex relationship between genetics and behavior. Arguing for a richly inter-active model, they point out that

> the process by which genes ultimately interact with each other, with various environmental factors, and at various levels of organization from the cell to the whole organism, are highly complex and subtle. We distort this complexity and subtlety, by making over-simplistic claims that are not substantiated by the data or methodologies at hand. (p. 9)

With these cautions in mind, I will consider a selection of research studies, popular reports, and anecdotes that propose to link biological markers and complex human behavior in causal chains. The purpose of this chapter will be to help to identify those presentations that deserve our attention in policymaking, those that do not, and why.

THE STORY OF CARRIE BUCK: PROBLEMATIC DEFINITIONS OF BEHAVIOR AND MARKERS

The first example of a link between complex human behavior and mark-ers is historical. It describes the destructive way in which class, gender, and hereditarian beliefs were joined in Virginia in the late 1920s. It is a story of the misapplication of the links between biological markers, complex human behavior, and social policy. In addition, the evidence presented in this historical case was so flawed that the reader must keep in mind the fact that it has no direct parallel to today's empirical research. Yet it does suggest the ways in which human wishes and attitudes can inform the way evidence is seen and used in policy decisions. It is the contemporary concern for the quality of evidence regarding markers and complex behavior, and the role of human expectations in its use, that leads to this chapter's caution.

The historical story in question concerns a young woman who was set upon by her guardians, by medical professionals, and by the law after having been judged a threat to America's genetic future. The young woman was Carrie Buck, the central litigant in the now-famous *Buck* v. *Bell* case of 1925.

Just 17 years old, poor, and pregnant as a consequence of rape, Buck had been placed, postpartum, in the Colony for Epileptics and Feebleminded in Lynchburg, Virginia. Her foster family, close relatives of the assailant in the rape, hoped to hide the attacker's identity from the general public and initiated her commitment. Thanks to the splendid historical work of Paul Lombardo (1985), we now know that Buck's internment represented a greater threat to the patient herself than admission to the Colony might have initially suggested. Lombardo reveals that the institute's superintendent, Dr. Albert Priddy, had been sterilizing patients under the guise of medical necessity for a number of years without legal justification. As luck would have it (and in this case the luck was all bad), Carrie's mother, Emma, had already been admitted to the Colony due in part to her status as a prostitute. This gave Priddy and his associates control over two of the three women they would require to make their case for legalizing forced sterilization by the state. The third candidate was Carrie's daughter, Vivian, who was then living with the original foster family.

The Buck case was corrupted from the start as the Colony's administration planned to use the court review of Carrie's proposed sterilization as a test case on the road to legalizing involuntary sterilizations. The prosecutor, the defense attorney, and the leadership of the Lynchburg School couldn't have been more collegial. Prosecuting the case against Buck was Director Priddy's colleague and old friend, Aubrey Strode. Speaking in Buck's defense was another of the director's long-time associates, and a member of the Colony's board that approved sterilizations, Mr. Irving Whitehead. By colluding on the Buck case, these men did all they could to assure that Priddy's legally questionable actions would be upheld. Their steps were well planned; first the case would have to be heard at the state level.

When Priddy's team came before the Amherst Virginia County Court in 1924, the charges against Buck were supported by some of America's leading eugenicists. In addition, the Colony called a local social worker to validate the mental limitations of Carrie's daughter, Vivian. The social worker identified Vivian's behavior as a reflection of the marker that had also tainted Carrie and Emma Buck. With remarkable powers of inference, Miss Wilhelm was able to describe 8-month-old Vivian as mentally challenged. "She has a look about [her] that is not quite normal," Wilhelm explained (Smith & Nelson, 1989, p. 108). With such problematic data in hand, Priddy's supporters were to tar all three generations with the marker of feeblemindedness. Even Carrie's lawyer was more loyal to the institution's interests than to Carrie's in that he seemed to have made "a deliberate decision not to defend [her]" (Lombardo, 1985, p. 51). Buck lost the case and the forced sexual sterilization of the feebleminded became a legal procedure in Virginia.

As often happens in cases concerning limitations on individual rights, the case moved to higher courts, and in April 1927 the Virginia decision was appealed to the federal level. On the second of May of that year the Virginia law was upheld by the U.S. Supreme Court using terminology that is remembered to this day. Speaking for the majority, Chief Justice Oliver Wendell Holmes balanced the general public good against the needs of the individual and warned of the danger of the heritability of criminal behavior.

> We have seen more than once, that the public welfare may call upon its best citizens for their lives. It would seem strange if it could not call upon those who already sap the strength of the State for their lesser sacrifices. . . . It is better for all the world, if instead of waiting to execute offspring for crime, [that] society prevent those who are manifestly unfit from continuing their kind. (U.S. Supreme Court Records, 1927, p. 207)

Reasoning from the state's ability to require vaccinations for its citizens, the Chief Justice penned the now famous words of the *Buck* v. *Bell* decision: "Three generations of imbeciles are enough" (U.S. Supreme Court Records, 1927, p. 207).

The success of Priddy's colleagues in defending the Virginia law at the national level set more than the standard for sterilization laws in the United States. It eventually became the model for forced state-sponsored sterilization in National Socialist Germany, giving the Buck story tragic implications of international proportions.

But the collusion of prosecution and defense was not the only issue that made the Buck case a miscarriage of justice. The issue was also one of empirical evidence and social attitudes. Even in 1927, evidence for the transmission of imbecility across three generations was problematic. That is, while Emma Buck, Carrie's mother, may have been mentally challenged, it was not clear that this was true for her daughter Carrie. Carrie after all had worked successfully for her foster family and had attended school for years before being sent to the Colony. In fact it was only in an attempt to protect the identity of her rapist that she was charged as feebleminded at all. Did the courts have irrefutable scientific evidence that she was a second generation in a line of congenitally feebleminded? Did they have genetic evidence that she was a carrier of some feebleminded quality predictably transmissible to her children? They did not.

And what of Carrie's daughter, Vivian? What do we know of that third generation? Actually the historical record provides fascinating information. We know that while Vivian may have been damned by the courts she was vindicated by the records of the Venable Elementary School of Charlottesville. Thanks to a careful analysis of her school records, we have compelling evidence of Vivian's normalcy. Indeed, Vivian "was a perfectly normal, quite average student, not particularly outstanding nor much troubled" (Gould, 1987, p. 316). If teachers' judgments may stand as a reasonable proxy for intellectual competence (and common practice suggests that they often do so), then we would do well to note that Vivian's report cards found her receiving "A's and B's for deportment and C's for all academic subjects but mathematics." More poignantly, Vivian was more than average; she was "placed on the honor roll in April [of] . . . 1931" (Gould, 1987, pp. 316–317).

If Carrie and Vivian were indeed damned by the courts, it was not based on hard evidence, but rather on the basis of ambiguous empirical markers. That is, there was no biological evidence at the time indicating that either of these women was a vector for socially destructive genetic qualities. But condemned they were by social proxies for hereditary worthlessness. As Toni Morrison (1970) might observe, the Buck women were condemned not so much for their heredity as for moving "at the hem of life" (p. 18).

The Carrie Buck case is a story of social injustice and determinist ideas, and perhaps no one has summarized that injustice more eloquently than Gould (1987), who notes that

> there were no imbeciles, not a one, among the three generations of Bucks, [and while] I don't know that such a correction of cruel but forgotten history counts for much, I find it both symbolic and satisfying to learn that forced eugenic sterilization, a procedure of such dubious morality, earned its justification (and won its most quoted line of rhetoric) on a patent falsehood. (pp. 317–318)

CURRENT RESEARCH ON COMPLEX
HUMAN BEHAVIOR AND GENETIC MARKERS

At this point we leave history behind in order to bring the discussion up to date, to bring it to a series of contemporary research studies that focus on human behavior in relation to its genetic underpinnings. We need to be clear as to the claims this chapter will make. First, the research studies under consideration are *not* further examples of the collusion that typified the Buck case. They are *not* examples of political activists' attempting to have their way with the uninformed and the dispossessed. Their only similarity with the Buck case, and this is of some moment, is that this research, linking complex human behavior with biological markers or their proxies, is still seen by many citizens as having an important role to play in public policy, and it continues to be open to the public's wishes and hereditarian hopes.

This chapter will make the point that except for cases of well-defined medical conditions linked to equally unambiguous markers, ties between human behavior and genetic substrates are far more complex than popular renderings would lead one to believe. Again, it is for reasons such as these that this chapter suggests caution.

If one follows reports in the popular press, genetic explanations for complex behaviors appear with striking regularity. Popular reports of behavior genetic and molecular genetic research seem to suggest that human traits, including an affinity for novelty (Angier, 1996); alcoholism (Reich, 1988); shyness (Kagen, 1993); homosexuality (Hamer et al., 1993); religiosity (Plomin, Owen, & McGuffin, 1994; Plomin, 1990); and child-rearing practices (Rushton, 1988) have significant genetic bases. Implicit in the popularization of these studies is the suggestion that the genetic markers for these behaviors either have been conclusively identified or are to be found shortly. Yet the issues involved in the public conversation about complex human behavior and markers are complicated to say the least. These issues include: (1) the categorization of the behavior and the markers in question; (2) the clarity of the definitions of these behaviors and markers; and (3) the presumed relationship between behavior and marker. Figure 7.1 lists a series of research studies of complex behavior and their associated statistical, genetic, and molecular markers. The discussion that follows will use this figure to facilitate an understanding of the studies and these three issues.

CATEGORIES OF BEHAVIORS

We begin the analysis with the Complex Behavior column of Figure 7.1. Here we want to distinguish between different *categories* of behavior. While some

Complex Behavior	*Marker*
Carrie Buck's Immorality	Feeblemindedness (Lombardo, 1985)
Tay-Sachs Disease	Recessive Gene (Kaback, 1977)
Criminality	Chromosomal Error -XYY, (Jacobs, 1965)
Down Syndrome	Chromosomal Error - Trisomy-21, (Smith, 1985)
Agreeableness	Similarity of Twins (Bouchard, 1989)
Alcoholism	D2 Receptor Gene (Blum, 1990)
Male Homosexuality	X Chromosome Marker (Hu, et al, 1995)
Love of Novelty	Survey Score/D4 Receptor (Angier, 1996)
Aggressive Behavior in Rats	Number of receptors in brain (Meaney, 1994)

FIGURE 7.1. Complex Human Behavior and Markers.

examples from this list are recognized as medically defined conditions, others derive their definitions primarily from social context. We err if we confuse these categories. The second example is for the medically defined condition Tay-Sachs disease. An individual with one recessive gene for the condition is a carrier for the condition while an individual with two genes for Tay-Sachs will present the condition. The third example is for criminality. Unlike Tay-Sachs, criminality is socially determined in ways in which genetically determined conditions are not. For example, in the late 1940s, the story of Audie Murphy's heroic World War II exploits were held up as a model of exemplary behavior; Murphy was credited with single-handedly wiping out a large number of German soldiers in battle. Obviously such behavior occurring in peacetime would have an entirely different meaning; the point is that its meaning is socially contingent. Unlike antisocial behavior, Tay-Sachs depends on medical, not social constructs for its identification. They are categorically different behaviors. Policymakers will not be able to thoughtfully consider the relationship between human behavior and markers (our third issue) if these different categories of behavior are confounded. Consumers of these studies must demand categorical clarity.

CLARITY OF BEHAVIORAL DEFINITIONS

In addition to categorical clarity, studies of behaviors and markers must also provide clear definitions of the behavior in question. But as Allen and

Futterman (1995) note, criminality turns out to be a highly ambiguous term. Indeed, the psychological community itself offers varying definitions of its meaning. It turns out to be what one might call a "moving target." Professional psychologists' solution to this problem has been to refine the definition of criminality as "antisocial behavior." But even that definition changes over time. Presenting evidence that underscores his point about ambiguous definitions, Futterman explains that antisocial behavior has had five different standard definitions over the past 20 years:

> Over two dozen changes have been made in the definition of antisocial personality disorder from . . . [1972 to 1994]. While some of these changes are apparently minor, . . . many others are more theoretically significant and suggest a different conception of the antisocial personality, e.g., the inclusion of a new manifestation of antisocial personality, "lack of remorse." (p. 54)

The point here is that different definitions of antisocial behavior will identify different individuals (phenotypes). Allen and Futterman warn that "prevalence rates . . . [for antisocial behavior] can differ by as much as 800% using different standard definitions in the same sample" (1995, p. 54). When the rates of a socially contingent complex human behavior vary by 800%, we are surely dealing with a "moving target." If such behavioral targets are hard to hit, consider the difficulty one must have in correlating them with markers. Here we can see how important clear definitions are to the policymaker and once again why caution is called for. The term *antisocial behavior* is just too ambiguous to serve as the basis for reasonable research programs or for sensible policy development.

Do these caveats concerning ambiguous definitions suggest that behavior and molecular geneticists should cease their research? Not at all. But when one considers the variety of phenotypes listed on the complex human behavior side of Figure 7.1 (immorality, criminality, Down Syndrome), one must demand clarity of definition. Linking behaviors to markers is a challenging endeavor, but if the behavioral targets move, the difficulty of the task is greatly increased. Clarity in definitions is necessary in all such studies. It is not always available.

CATEGORIES OF MARKERS

We turn now to the right column of Figure 7.1, to a consideration of markers. As with the discussion of behaviors, the concern begins with the categorical clarity of the markers. As we can see, markers can be IQ test scores, chromosomes, the statistical similarity of siblings or family members, radioactive markers on the DNA, or genes themselves. The point here is that they are not samples from equivalent categories. One might think of these markers in terms of levels, ranging from high-inference markers, as in the Carrie Buck case, to low-inference markers, as in the XYY karyotype. Consumers of this research would do well not to confuse these markers in their review of behavior and molecular genetic studies. The studies vary on conceptual and methodological grounds depending on the nature of the marker under consideration. As in the behavioral and social sciences, differences in methods and objects of study can often distinguish one's membership in a field itself. Not all researchers looking for relationships between human behavior and markers are doing the same thing. There are significant differences between the data and methods of behavioral and molecular geneticists. We need to remain sensitive to them.

CLARITY OF THE MARKERS

As with the requirement that definitions of complex behaviors be clear, so too must the definitions of the markers be unambiguous. They must be clearly identified and consistently linked to the behavior under study if they are to be part of the policymaking process. If the marker serves as a proxy, as it did in the Carrie Buck example, it must unambiguously represent its genetic substrate. But as we saw in that historical example, judgments of intellectual capacity were so fraught with cultural bias that correlations between feeblemindedness and out-of-wedlock births ended up saying remarkably little about genetic causality. Further, given the nature of the controls in that example, such judgments (even if put into IQ test score language) would have served as poor proxies for the genetic inheritance of the three generations in question. But today's molecular geneticists use quite sophisticated techniques and deal with far different kinds of markers. When these markers are at the level of the chromosome, as is the case of Down Syndrome, and XYY phenotypes, marker ambiguity is significantly reduced.

UNAMBIGUOUS CHROMOSOMAL MARKERS
FOR COMPLEX BEHAVIOR: TRISOMY-21

In order to underscore the importance of clear definitions, we now consider two examples that link complex behavior to markers at the level of the chromosome. The following studies link complex human behavior to unambiguously defined markers at the level of the chromosome. We begin with a discussion of Down Syndrome, and then move to studies that link

XYY chromosomes and criminality. As we shall see, even though both studies identify unambiguously defined markers, both studies do not guarantee rigorous links between behavior and marker. It is only in the first case that such a warranted empirical conclusion can be drawn.

Down Syndrome was named for the British physician Dr. John L. H. Down after he carefully described it in 1866, avoiding the racially tinged nomenclature Mongolian Idiocy. It is, however, associated with the presence of three chromosomes rather than two at the 21st location of the human karyotype. During cell division the human chromatic material splits in half. In some small percentage of cases, a meiotic error or nondisjunction occurs during the production of eggs or sperm (a failure of the chromatic material to split during reduction division) and the resulting cells carry additional chromatic material. If this material is associated with the 21st chromosome during fertilization, then all the cells of the resulting zygote—except for red blood cells, which have no nucleus—will have an extra 21st chromosome. Ergo, Trisomy-21.

It is interesting to know that the chromosomal basis for Down Syndrome was not discovered until 1959, and we still know little about why this error occurs (Gould, 1980, pp. 160–168). But we do know that any individual having the Trisomy-21 error will express Down Syndrome to some degree. The condition has been unambiguously described in the medical literature and, as we have seen above, its marker is easily identified through karyotype analysis. In every case, the individual will express symptoms. Trisomy-21 studies supply us with evidence that links unambiguously defined chromosomal markers and unambiguously defined human behavior (Cicchetti & Beeghly, 1990; Smith, 1985).

AMBIGUOUS BEHAVIORAL MARKERS: XYY CHROMOSOMES AND CRIMINAL BEHAVIOR

There are other studies that have identified unambiguous chromosomal markers but have had far less success in attempting to make links to complex human behavior. Studies linking criminal behavior and XYY chromosomes serve as examples here; as it turns out, while the marker is unambiguous the behavior is not.

All normal human male body cells have an XY chromosome pair; human females have an XX pair. In 1965, 4 years after a male with an XYY karyotype had been identified, a study of 197 male prisoners found that they presented the XYY condition at nearly twice the expected rate. Scientists hypothesized that the inmate's violent behavior might have been caused by the additional Y chromosome (Allen & Futterman, 1995, p. 37).

Reports of the research gained considerable publicity and additional studies of incarcerated males followed. As "more examples of XYY males were uncovered it began to appear that the frequency of XYY males in at least some penal institutions appeared to be significantly higher that the frequency estimated for the general population" (Allen & Futterman, 1995, p. 37). For some observers, the cause of the violent behavior seemed to have been found. It was presumed that the extra Y caused violent behavior in the same way that Trisomy-21 caused Down Syndrome. Some researchers considered the possibility that an increase in male hormones might lead to violence, while others suggested that increased growth at puberty might make the subjects bigger than average and therefore prone to hyper-activity. Yet others suggested that "the extra Y chromosome specifically affected brain development, acting on 'violence centers' supposed to exist in areas such as the hypothalamus or amygdala" (Allen & Futterman, 1995, p. 38). Despite these interesting hypotheses, the exact way in which the extra Y influenced behavior was not known.

While the presence of a single explanatory mechanism remained elusive, it did not reduce the desire to link crime to a genetic substrate. As Allen and Futterman (1995) note, "despite the lack of a specific mechanism,"

> by the mid-1960s some researchers were convinced that there could well be a direct link between possession of an XYY chromosome complement and a person's chances of being a criminal. (p. 38)

Others were far more cautious in drawing such conclusions. For example, when two Johns Hopkins University researchers analyzed the XYY research, they found the studies wanting on both substantive and methodological grounds. They judged them unconvincing (Borogoankar & Shah, 1974). While XYY inmates were supposed to be more violent than their XY counterparts, the XYY prison cohort was actually found to be more cooperative than the XY group. Further, physiological and psychological profiles did not distinguish XYY and XY males. Yes, the XYY prisoners were slightly taller than their XY counterparts, but comparative skeletal structure, electrocardiogram, electroencephalogram, and skin trait analyses found the XYY subjects to be average for those qualities. In fact, as Borogoankar and Shah noted,

> the IQ of XYY males appear[ed] to be about the mean for inmates of penal institutions. No significant differences in personality traits distinguish[ed] XYY's from XY's. In short, by all significant physical or psychological criteria that might affect behavior, XYY males rate about the same as XY males. (p. 48)

The studies were also found to have procedural flaws; they often lacked matched samples of XYY and XY subjects, blind or double-blind controls, and standardized data-collection procedures. The point here is that it is difficult to attribute genetic cause to complex behavior when environmental factors are ignored. "Inadequate understanding of the phenomena and the premature conclusions about the XYY phenotype which have been reported with distressing frequency," the Hopkins scientists warned, "have produced remarkably simplistic views of the interactions between XYY genotypes and the almost infinitely varied environments with which they interact." With comments that apply to today's studies of genetics and crime, they continued,

> We should always keep in mind that even the demonstration of a genetic contribution to impulse control warrants only the conclusion that in certain environments some persons with particular genotypes will respond by developing certain behavioral problems more frequently than others. However, this does not preclude the possibility that in some other environments persons with the very same genotypes . . . may well manifest socially adaptive behavior. (Borogoankar & Shah, 1974, p. 205)

In keeping with the analytic frame of Figure 7.1, while XYY studies were able to identify unambiguously a chromosomal anomaly (marker), they failed to define unambiguously the complex behavior in question. The behavioral target moved. As a consequence, these studies of criminality are unable to enlighten policymakers concerning the role an additional Y chromosome might play in criminal behavior.

COMMONSENSE LINKS BETWEEN
BEHAVIOR AND MARKER: SKELETON SLEDDING

Studies of Trisomy-21 and XYY cast light on the third issue in the critique of research on complex behavior and markers. They focus our attention on the relationship between behavior and marker. We need to know the nature of the relationship if there is one. Is it correlative? Causal? Interactive? For scientists and policymakers the answers to these questions are critical. While the coexistence of behavior and marker is of some interest, interactive or causal relationships are judged to be the basis for policymaking; the nature of the relationship matters. In the case of Trisomy-21 the causal relationship was supported by the data. While the XYY studies also presumed causality, methodological limitations kept cautiously skeptical researchers from rejecting the null hypothesis. No causal relationship exists between criminal behavior and the extra Y chromosome.

I do not mean to suggest with the above discussion that human behavior has no genetic component. Of course it does. And further, in cases such as Down Syndrome and others, genetics does indeed determine a range of behavior. But in the case of complex human behavior, which is always the result of the dialectic of nature and nurture, the behavior-marker relationship is far more complicated than it might initially appear. Heredity may not be the causative factor for the behavior in question. Some critics even go so far as to argue that attempts to separate nature and nurture in complex human behavior will prove to be an impossibility (Wasserman, 1996).

In addition, commonsense explanations of daily events often distort our understanding of the relationship between behaviors and markers by implying causal relationships where none exist. Consider, for example, the way in which the *New York Times* reported on the competitor in the new sport of skeleton sledding. Skeleton sledding is akin to riding on the Flexible Flyer sled of one's youth, but with significant differences. The skeleton sled is heavy, luge-like, and propels its rider downhill, head-first, at speeds of 80 miles per hour. The *Times* reported on Jim Shea of Lake Placid, New York, a likely medal winner who has the advantage of sledding on home ice. Practice, in this case, might make perfect. But that was not all—and here is where the distortions of our commonsense renderings of the importance of heredity come into play. "In addition to a geographical edge," the article explains, Mr. Shea had "a genetic advantage as well." Assuming the relationship between heredity and behavior to be causal, the *Times* further points out that the genetic advantage was inherited. It seems that "Shea's grandfather, Jack, won two gold medals in speed skating in the 1932 Winter Olympics, and his father, Jack Jr., was a Nordic combined skier for the 1964 United States Winter Olympic Team" (Gould, 1996, p. B 15). Jim Shea certainly shares genes with his father and grandfather. Indeed, the specific percentages of their genetic contribution is easily determined by any high school biology student. But Shea also shares a common environment with his father and grandfather. It's an environment that highly values active winter sports. The idea that skating, skiing, and sledding may be caused by a common genetic substrate may be commonsensical, but it seems far from an easily verifiable genetic finding. Indeed, one need not be an environmental determinist to recognize that geographic location and family pressure might well account for Mr. Shea's high speed Olympic antics, genetics notwithstanding.

QUALITY, CLARITY, AND RELATIONSHIP: THE HYPOTHETICAL BASEBALL CAP CASE

The hereditarian attitudes and interpretations expressed on the pages of the *New York Times* are not without a supportive context, however. After all, some molecular geneticists do approach family trait studies in a roughly similar fashion.

Let me share a hypothetical story that may help the reader better to understand this chapter's cautions regarding the role of such social attitudes in explanations of complex human behavior. Here is how that molecular argument is constructed. First, one identifies a group of men who have a specific complex behavior in common. It could be antisocial behavior or down-hill sledding. But this hypothetical story will focus on something far less serious: the wearing of baseball caps in a backwards fashion. Having identified a common behavior, one then searches for a common genetic marker in the genomes of these men. Finding such a marker, given the 3 billion base pairs that make up the human DNA strand's 50,000 to 100,000 genes, should not be an impossibility. A common marker is found in the genomes of these men and a causal but I believe flawed chain of explanation follows. The marker is presumed to code for neuroanatomical changes in male brains. These common changes, given American youth's fascination with sports, predispose men to wear reversed baseball caps. The popular explanation? Genes play an important role in the choice of haberdashery. While the example is of course a silly and strained one, the logic it employs can be found in numerous neurogenetic explanations of complex human behavior.

GENES FOR THE LOVE OF NEW THRILLS

Consider the example of the popular media's interpretation of the finding that a gene had been discovered that coded for human "novelty seeking" (Angier, 1996, p. A1). The findings were initially reported by teams of scientists from the National Institutes of Health and the Sarah Herzog Memorial Hospital in Jerusalem (Hamer et al., 1993). Having administered a self-report questionnaire to subjects in both Israel and the United States who were also tested for the presence of the gene in question, the researchers found a statistically significant correlation between the presence of the gene and high-scoring subjects on the questionnaire. The researchers explain the relationship between behavior and marker using a logic similar to the baseball cap example.

They explain that the gene in question codes for the increased production of dopamine uptake receptors in the human brain. Dopamine is thought to be associated with human pleasure seeking and in this case it is correlated with reports that individuals enjoy searching for new experiences. The gene codes for novelty seeking. Or does it? I must admit that the empiricist in me finds this explanation somewhat incomplete. But we want to be careful here, for just as in the cap example above, there is a neurogenetic association with all human behavior. That association is not being denied.

Rather, the issue this research raises, and about which one needs to be cautious, is that of the kind of relationship that exists between the marker and the behavior.

The presumption that the genes played a significant role in influencing novelty seeking may be open to alternative interpretations. It is quite possible to locate all the pieces that these researchers have found and to create an entirely different explanatory puzzle. And research done by McGill University's Michael Meaney may permit us to do so.

INCREASING DOPAMINE RECEPTORS IN THE BRAINS OF RATS

Meaney (1994) works not with human risk-taking behavior but with rats and their reaction to stress. While finding a correlation between marker and behavior is important, Meaney points out that "it is only a first step" (quoted in Begley, 1996, p. 57). He offers a compelling alternative explanation in which it is the environment that influences neurological structure rather than one in which genes determine behavior. It is an explanation that provides us with just the sort of empirical data for behavior-marker relationships that the above sledding and novelty-seeking examples seem to be lacking.

Meaney's work (1994) suggests that while genes are surely a factor in explaining complex behavior, they are not necessarily the significant factor. As with the baseball cap and novelty-seeking examples, Meaney's experiments provide the reader with data at the levels of behavior, marker, and neuroreceptor. But rather than describing a causal chain in which genes shape neurological structure, which in turn determines behavior, Meaney finds that it is the organism's environment that affects the chemistry of neurotransmission. It is environment that changes the brain.

Meaney (1994) was able to alter the number of receptors in the rats' brains for specific chemicals by separating pairs of newborn rats from their mothers and varying the stress levels of their environments (Begley, 1996, p. 57). "The rats that were stressed as pups had fewer of certain receptors [as adults] and so tended to overproduce stress hormones; normal rats had more receptors and were less likely to be flooded with hormones during stress" (p. 57). To repeat, here we have research that links behavior, neurotransmitters, and genes in a logical chain that makes environment the causal factor.

Could we extrapolate from stressing rats to human novelty seeking and still maintain Meaney's logic? I believe that the answer is yes. Consider the case of childhood traumatic experiences. "Might certain childhood experiences," for example, "being menaced by a new dog, falling from a new

Jungle-Gym—determine whether one develops more or fewer brain receptors for novelty seeking?"

> All it would take is a mechanism like the one Meaney found. . . . Early life experiences were so influential in the rats . . . that they literally determined which receptor genes turned on, and thus how many receptors the brain built. (Begley, 1996, p. 57)

The reader would be wrong to see this research as an apologia for a new sort of environmental determinism. It is not. But it does strongly suggest that policymakers who blame the poor, the criminal, and the disenfranchised for their own conditions might reconsider their policies in light of these findings.

As educators, we recognize that human beings are learners. We further understand that through a process of nonadaptive evolutionary change, the human brain has become predisposed to learn. And so we strongly support the proposition that the potentiality for such complex behavior as learning has a neurogenetic substrate or marker. But as Meaney's research (1994) so clearly points out, it is the experiences that we provide to our students in the form of education and cultural access that enhance that potentiality. It is the pedagogical environments that we create that influence achievement. Indeed it is these very experiences that develop our students' competence, in a material sense (recall, the actual number of receptors in the brains of the rats were changed by their environment). In sum, we are responsible for the richness or poverty of that environment. Blaming the victim for his or her hereditary affliction on genetic grounds may be scientifically baseless (Brooks-Dunn, Klebanov, & Duncan, 1996). As University of Maryland bioethicist David Wasserman (1996) notes,

> neurogenetic research focused on individual differences is unlikely to yield genuine insight into the causes of . . . [complex human] behavior, but it is likely to discover markers and genes that are loosely associated with that behavior. (p. 108)

And such loose associations, such loose relationships between behavior and marker as noted in the case of XYY chromosomes and criminality, are a cause for caution. The discovery of such loosely associated markers and behaviors, Wasserman continues, "will be highly susceptible to abuse by agencies of social control, from schools to parole boards, because those markers and genes will be easy to detect, and tempting to employ in programs of screening and preemptive intervention" (p. 108). For human service professionals and policymakers, the future will require caution and careful understanding if our clients' needs are to be met authentically.

GENETIC DETERMINISM AND SEXUAL ORIENTATION

Interestingly enough, victim-blaming can often become so internalized that the victims themselves take on the role of oppressor. The issue of the relationship between behavior and marker is the focus of our discussion and it should be noted that it has caused a serious debate in the gay community as well (Byne, 1994; Gorman, 1995; Hamer et al., 1993; LaVay & Hamer, 1994; Risch et al., 1993). Consider the position of those within the community who argue that the basis for homosexuality and sexual orientation in general is biologically determined—that "gayness" is determined by one's genes. The presumed relationship is causal, from gene to behavior.

For some observers of the debate on the causes of sexual orientation, this position seems to reflect a form of false consciousness. It is a false consciousness in which those who are despised for their differences embrace the determinism of biology as a potential defense against bias. It can be a dangerous defense. As Stephen Rose (1995) notes, "this 'victim blaming' generates in its turn a sort of fatalism among those it stigmatizes; it is not our fault [some gay individuals argue], the problem lies in our biology. Such fatalism," he continues, "can bring its own relief, for less stigma attaches to being the carrier or transmitter of deficit genes, than to having been morally responsible. It is striking," Rose observes,

> that in the United States, leading gay activists have embraced the gay brain/gay genes explanation for their sexual orientation on the explicit grounds that they can no longer be held morally culpable for a "natural" state, nor can they be seen as dangerously likely to infect others with their "perverse" tastes. (p. 382)

Rose's point is that if homosexuality is not genetically determined, then gay men are again socially at risk. This does appear a dangerous political gambit.

There is another argument used by members of the gay community to explain homosexuality in biological terms and it seems problematic as well. Cast in historical-genetic terms, this argument points to the presumed advantages that accrued to the nearest relatives of the earliest homosexual *homo sapiens*. In this argument, the "gay genes" in a family line gave that family a survival advantage over families lacking such genes and individuals. That is, having a gay male sibling who did not father children (and who has gay genes), but who could hunt and offer the community protection, gave one's clan the advantage of his extra hunting and defending hands. The genes were in the family line and the presence of an occasional gay family member could be depended on and would be valued. As a consequence, the relatives of those gay men would have an increased chance of survival and would produce more offspring, offspring who would be carriers of gay genes. Gayness therefore had an evolutionary advantage and must be recognized for its importance today.

The problem with all such stories, however, is that they are stories. Other contradictory stories could easily be told and they would be equally plausible. If homosexuality is not determined in a strong sense, then the families of our ancient forebearers *did not* receive an advantage from having nonparent food providers in the clan (perhaps they wouldn't hunt). Following on from this story, today's gay men lose their historical and contemporary raison d'être. In addition, if the scientific evidence shows that gayness is not determined by genetics, then homosexuals loose their genetic "protection" from those who would ostracize them. These are dangerous legitimation strategies.

Perhaps a more reasonable explanation for gayness is to argue that a percentage of the population learns to express sexuality in exclusively homosexual ways. But this choice is not genetically determined in a strong sense. Humans are predisposed to being sexual, one might argue, and all we know for sure is that this predisposition takes many forms. Legitimating one's sexuality through historical anecdotes and on the basis of ambiguous genetic data, rather than on the strong evidence of human variation, can be dangerous indeed.

THE NONSEPARABILITY OF NATURE AND NURTURE: TWIN STUDIES AND COVARIANCE EFFECTS

Now molecular geneticists, considering the above discussion, might respond that genetics still has a very significant role to play in human behavior. They might argue that the plasticity in the number of receptors in rats' and human brains is within a norm of reaction for the expression of that gene. The number can be high or low in relation to environment. This is a compelling insight. It is this range in the number of brain receptors, these researchers argue, not the behavior itself, that is genetically determined. They might then argue that work such as that of Meaney (1994) simply reflects two possibilities from such a constrained range. They might conclude that it is the coding for the range that is hereditary—that is, specific genes code for the range of behaviors that underlie homosexual or criminal behavior. In that sense the behaviors are caused by the genes.

For behavior geneticists, building on the insights of their molecular colleagues, the research task is to identify the amount of an organism's performance (whether it be novelty-seeking, brain receptor–driven activity, or sexual preference) that can be attributed to environment and the amount that can be attributed to heredity. Here the task is to parse out the individual contributions that nature and nurture make in complex behavior. When this is the task, research often focuses on sets of identical twins as subjects of study (Gottesman & Goldsmith, in press). Since identical twins' genetic inheritance is equal, separation at birth into completely different contexts should make any differences in their behavior attributable to environment. In theory at least, twins that have been separated at birth and placed into differing environments should serve as highly reliable subjects for detecting genetic traits.

As Paul Billings and his colleagues point out in their critical analysis of neurogenetic determinism, twin studies "are . . . used to support the hypothesis concerning the hereditary basis of a trait" (Billings, Beckwith, & Alper, 1992, p. 228). Since caution is the leitmotiv of this chapter, we will focus on some of the limitations that Billings and his associates associate with those studies.

An initial limitation of twin studies concerns the presumed differences in the environments in which twins are brought up. Reliable twin studies require significantly differing environments for the separated siblings, but often differences are not found. Citing the work of Leon Kamin (1974, 1993) and others, Billings and colleagues (1992) point out that the environments in the majority of twin studies, rather than being significantly different, are remarkably alike. The explanation here is straightforward. Separated twins are often placed in the homes of relatives; they often remain in the same town, and they often go to the same schools. In addition, professional adoption agencies often try to "match" adoptive parents to their adoptees, resulting in very similar, rather than different, environments for the separated twins. Simply put, these environments are just not that dissimilar. Perhaps one should not be surprised when researchers report, with the seeming validation of the popular press, that identical genomes and dissimilar environments produce twins who have a selection of complex behaviors in common. Do such studies provide us with evidence that their common genes (markers) substantively caused their common complex behavior? It would not seem so. The methodological requirement, that similar genomes be placed in differing environments, had not been met.

A second limitation of twin studies is the issue of selecting the twins themselves. Cohorts of twins are often contacted through notices in newspapers and magazines. Those who respond are in a very real sense self-selected. As a consequence, they do not represent a random sample from the entire set of twins in a population. Billings and colleagues (1992) point out,

Those twins who do respond to news coverage may represent a biased population who, for example, have a particular interest in "being twins" and so
more closely resemble each other than would a more randomly ascertained
cohort. (p. 229)

Gould (1993) adds to the critique of twin studies an additional caveat about
sample size. He notes that although a few pairs of twins do report some
peculiar behavior in common, there are thousands of pairs who have never
made it into the studies at all (p. 10). Their dissimilar behavior goes un-
recorded. That some small percentage of a population of identical twins
has personality traits in common is indeed of interest and it may be worthy
of study, but it is hardly a compelling reason to presume that genes play a
significant role in determining complex behavior.

Nevertheless, twin studies continue to be a popular approach to the
challenge of disaggregating nature and nurture. While some in the research
community might find the limitations overwhelming, this has not been true
for all. The well-known Minnesota Twin Studies, for example, have produced a series of "startling similarities in behavior between identical twins
who had been reared apart." Included here are "flushing the toilet twice,
sneezing in elevators, wearing cowboy hats and wearing seven rings" (Billings et al., 1992, p. 229). Not surprisingly, reports of these common behaviors regularly receive broad press coverage.

These remarkable findings might well cause the reader to wonder what
possible markers the researchers could provide in association with the
complex behaviors. The answer, which necessarily is cast in terms of the
statistical similarities between phenotypes (twins), actually says nothing
directly about genetic markers. The careful reader will find no reference
to additional chromosomal material or recessive genes in these behavior
genetic studies of toilet flushing, ring wearing, and sneezing in the lift. This
highlights an important distinction between studies in behavioral genetics and those in molecular genetics. Where the behavior geneticist focuses
on inferred similarities between phenotypes, it is the molecular geneticist
who uses the "newer approaches employing DNA linkage methods [which]
can lead to the complete biochemical identification of a gene linked to a
human phenotype which is inherited in a simple Mendelian manner" (Billings et al., 1992, p. 228). To place this point in the terms of our earlier discussion, the measured marker in behavior genetic studies of twins is never
genetic; it is always a statement of statistical similarity. Even though genetic identity is understood in these studies of twins, their genetic makeup
is never plumbed directly.

Although some critics find this reason enough to conclude that twin
studies offer no convincing evidence of the genetic basis of human behav-

ior, it should be clear to the reader that the types of evidence offered in molecular and behavioral genetic studies are not the same (Billings et al., 1992, p. 228). Once again, the statistical similarity of twins' behavior is quite different from an assay of a gene itself. While these differing markers may or may not serve as convincing evidence for the behaviors in question, we err if we confuse them.

Having made the point that behavior genetic studies of twins are statistical rather than molecular, let us consider an additional limitation of these studies that attempt to disaggregate nature and nurture. This fourth limitation concerns the presence of what statisticians call "covariance effects." Some critics of twin studies argue that due to covariance effects, nature and nurture cannot be separated. As a consequence of this nonseparation, behavior-genetic studies can never determine the amount of the variance of a complex human behavior that can be attributed to an individual's genetics or to his or her environment.

Put in everyday language, the way we look (being Asian, African American, or Mediterranean, for example) influences the way the environment treats us and we cannot separate these factors in individual development. A person's social experience is often influenced by the environment's response to his or her appearance. In the case of twins, common physical attributes increase the similarity of their social environments. That is, identical twins' identical genetic makeup creates similar environments within which they develop.

When thinking of social environments, one might consider the ways in which American society has constructed the ideal form for the human body. In North America, where anxiety about weight has made an industry out of dieting, it seems safe to say that a person's weight will influence the way in which that person is treated. In addition,

> individuals who are considered attractive can share common developmental experiences, as may those who are deemed ugly. Women and members of certain racial groups experience discrimination based upon appearance. Therefore, identical twins, looking alike, may tend to be treated in a similar manner. (Billings et al., 1992, p. 230)

We're talking about covariance effects here and it might be better to unpack the issue through a story. It is a story that will challenge the presumption that reared-apart twins enjoy significantly different environments.

We begin this story with identical twins separated at birth. They are both male. And of course they look alike. By their 16th birthday they are both tall (attaining a height of 6'3") and they both have flaming red hair. Would their strikingly similar appearance garner similar social responses? It would seem so. Indeed, these similar responses to their appearance could lead our tall redheaded twins to develop similar personality traits that are not related to the direct influence of their common genes. It may be that their common heredity has influenced their environments rather than their behaviors. This may still appear a bit abstract, so let us see how this interaction might play out in a more specific example.

Size does make a difference in the lives of children; tall children are more likely to be picked first for basketball teams than their shorter classmates. In addition, for many parents and coaches there is an expectation that tall youngsters will play the game well. Further, redheads, unlike brunettes or blondes, are more than likely to be given the obvious nickname "Red" (no surprise here). Having such a slang moniker will probably increase the public's ability to recognize them. Let us also assume that, when the public is questioned about the personality traits of redheaded people, their common answer is number two below:

> "Redheaded people often have a (_____) personality."
> 1. calm   2. volatile   3. loving   4. aloof

If the above expectations are an accepted part of our social fabric, then our twins will probably develop in contexts that positively reinforce a deep involvement in sports as well as what psychologists call "acting out" behavior. Unless social psychologists are entirely wrong, such expectations should bear behavioral fruit.

Indeed we know enough from the literature on self-fulfilling prophecies and school achievement to understand that such expectations have consequences. While our twins might have been separated at birth, they could come together to compete at basketball. In such an imaginary world, one would not be surprised to overhear opposing middle-school basketball coaches advising their players to "watch out for that tall redheaded center ('Red' Smith or 'Red' Jones respectively) since he's good and he's got a really short temper." In this story, at least, the opposing players would do well to heed the advice.

Placing this story in the context of behavior genetics one might well ask, "Did the twins' shared genes make them aggressive basketball players?" The answer is an unambiguous no. We have no evidence of genetic markers that code for aggressive lay-ups. A far more reasonable and verifiable hypothesis suggests that it was the social responses to the twins' common physical attributes that served to influence their behavior. Speaking to just this issue, Billings and colleagues (1992) note that "the identical genes that twins harbor . . . [create] similar environments even when the twins [grow] up in different locations" (p. 230). In our study, it was not the twins' common genes, although they certainly have them, that caused the similar behavior. It was social expectations created by the twins' identical height and hair color that nurtured the behaviors in question. The "similar personality traits [of the twins] would be *associated* with shared genes (particularly those for physical appearance) but not *caused* by identical 'personality genes'" (p. 230, emphasis in original). The genes for red hair and above-average height did not create the personalities of our aggressive basketball centers. Their similar North American social contexts, together with these qualities, reinforced the behavior. Returning to the topic that began this discussion and to the mathematical rather than the molecular nature of behavior-genetic studies, "such associations have been defined in the statistics literature as 'covariance effects' and [they] are not uncommon" (p. 230).

I would agree with the critics' point that not only are covariance effects common, but that they also represent an important issue for those studying research that attempts to disaggregate nature and nurture. I further agree with the position that holds that in these studies, genes and environments are inextricably intertwined. The equation is not one of three factors in which nature plus nurture equals behavior. It is rather an equation composed of four factors in which the dynamic interaction of nature and nurture creates inseparable covariance effects that result in the twins' complex behavior. This four-factor model includes nature, environment, covariance effects, and complex behavior. The key point here is that such integrations, such covariance effects, cannot be reduced to either genes or environment.

"Surely," the reader must be thinking, "there are hereditary and environmental factors that directly influence the phenotype and that fit within the three-factor model." That is correct. On the one hand we have *hereditary* errors that cause phenotypic errors such as Phenylketonuria. And infants with this metabolic error must be given a special diet from birth if they are not to be severely limited as adults. On the other hand, an environment that is bereft of protein will have an equally profound impact on a developing fetus or neonate. But when behavior geneticists search for the causes of *complex human behavior*, this three-factor paradigm is not helpful. As our prior stories and Figure 7.2 explain, while genes and environment can have direct effects, their primary and overarching influence in complex human behavior is that of their interaction, that of covariance effects.

As Figure 7.2 illustrates, the interaction of expressed genes (e.g., tall redheaded males) and environment (e.g., expectations for aggressive basketball playing) is inseparable and represents a third factor in the equation. The complex behavior described in our story comes as a result of this

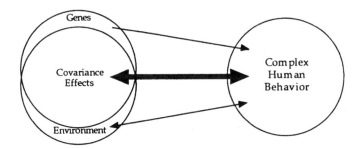

FIGURE 7.2. Covariance Effects and Complex Human Behavior.

integration of factors. Speaking to this issue, Billings and his associates (1992) conclude:

> We believe that the interaction between genes and environmental factors that produce covariant effects should likely be considered as a third category not reducible to either genetics or environment. If it is true, that most of human behavior results from a complex interplay between genetics and environment and thus falls into this other category, [then] it would be very misleading to argue, as [some behavior geneticists] seem to be doing, that most of human behavior is genetically, as opposed to environmentally influenced. (p. 230)

Once again, the point here is not to choose sides in a debate between the determinism of either nature or nurture. The point is to caution against such false positions and to recognize the inseparability of these factors in human development.

CONCLUSION

The above litany of cautions has not been offered from the perspective of a genetic Neo-Luddite. In our roles as educators and citizens we must carefully thread our way between the shoals of a naive acceptance of biological determinism ("markers for a certain human medical condition have been found so all of our behavior must be determined by our genes") and a mindless rejection of scientific evidence ("biological explanations of human behavior are irrelevant and 'politically incorrect'"). Discussions of the research linking genetics and complex human behavior are typified by both consensus and controversy. The issues of definition, clarity, and covariance effects raised in this chapter were not presented for the purpose of rejecting the research under consideration. On the contrary, in identifying areas of agreement, Wasserman (1996) notes that

> virtually all the participants in the debate [concerning complex human be-
> havior and its putative markers] recognize the difficulties posed for genetic
> research by poor definition, heterogeneous nature, and social construction
> of the "phenotype" of [socially destructive] behavior; the importance of tak-
> ing environmental variables into account in assessing genetic influences; the
> limited explanatory value of statistical studies of heritability; [and] the dan-
> ger of treating "genetic" as "immutable." (p. 1)

This chapter should be seen as located in that professional community of discourse. It is just those consensus issues of categorization, clarity of definitions, and the relationship between behavior and marker that have served as the basis for this cautionary tale.

Wasserman (1996) concludes that an additional point of agreement for researchers and critics alike, and potentially the most important issue, is the consensus that exists around the "urgency of preventing human genetic research from being used for eugenic and racist purposes" (p. 1). This last area of agreement brings us back to the discussion that began this general analysis and this book. The sense of urgency that all of us feel reflects our historical recognition of the destructive uses to which biological determinism had been put in the past.

Biological determinism served as a key link in the chain of eugenics. As the research on eugenics and American education reveals, the Popular Eugenics Movement was strong and effective during the first half of this century. Its national organizations sponsored meetings, congresses, and exhibitions popularizing the eugenic ideal of human betterment through controlled breeding and as a movement it was also supported by many of the intellectual leaders of the day.

Supporters of Eugenics included Edward Lee Thorndike, perhaps the nation's most prominent leader in educational measurement, and Leta Hollingworth, an early and articulate supporter of education for gifted and talented youth. Our professional organizations also played a role. For example, the National Education Association formally sponsored the Committee on Racial Well-being, which expressed a decidedly eugenic turn of mind in its policy prescriptions. As we now know, despite an articulate resistance to its principles and practices, the eugenics credo penetrated both teacher training and high school science textbooks during the interwar years. It is a knowledge of this history that has informed this cautionary tale regarding the potential misuses of the findings of the behavior-genetic research on complex human behavior today.

It is clear to proponents and critics alike that research into complex human behavior does indeed raise many of the same issues that concerned early American eugenicists. But there is no need for us to fall again into the ideological quagmire of that earlier period. The eugenicists' error was to ignore the best scientific studies and evidence of their day and to let their hereditarian social attitudes distort their understandings of that science. By so doing, they lost touch with developments in genetics and simply became political actors. In an unwitting way, they allowed for the capturing of science by particular ideological interests.

Thanks to the critical literature that has developed as a response to that history, we are no longer as easily prone to such errors. Today's critical work serves as a corrective to such tendencies. That critical work permits us to support the potentially important findings of today's molecular geneticists, while at the same time critically interpreting the unwarranted assertions of today's biological determinists. For those who would see today's research into complex human behavior and its markers as a prelude to a new determinist eugenics, we would caution against inappropriate understanding of those findings. However, remembering that past and defending against inappropriate interpretations of today's research may not be enough. Some take a much stronger rejectionist position, contending that

> genetic and/or neurogenetic explanations of [complex human behavior] are seriously flawed by any of the canons of modern scientific research. They are flawed conceptually . . . they are flawed methodologically [and] . . . most important, they are flawed as guides for social decisions. (Allen & Futterman, 1995, p. 4)

If this be true, then what should guide our social policy decisions? What should those of us committed to the future of America's schoolchildren do in light of the history of the Popular Eugenics Movement and of today's debates about the role of genetics in complex human performance? Again, I believe that the answer is quite clear. Human beings are indeed animals. We do indeed come into this world with a genetic past. But that past must not be seen in the form of determinations. It must rather be seen in terms of potentialities. And this is not merely a social or political ideal. It comes from a careful reading of the science of the case itself. Whether one considers contemporary scientific research or the continuing work of America's teachers with children of every background, it is the development of the human organism's potential that serves as the subtext for our professional lives. It is the subtext for our policymaking as well.

As noted before, we are about the business of maximizing potentials. That task requires that we pay attention to both the potential of our youth and to those forces that would limit their future. Limited material support in health, housing, personal security, and education surely limits this potential. But a set of unwarranted determinist ideas can be equally limiting. Such ideas can be driven more by the need to believe than by the need to know, and in the early 20th century eugenics was supported by such believers.

As a consequence of our understanding of the historical record of eugenics and its destructive effects, we can avoid repeating the eugenicists' errors. By understanding legitimate cautions regarding research on complex human behavior and markers, we can choose the findings that are appropriate and avoid those of limited usefulness. Molecular genetics is not eugenics and the search for markers for complex behavior may not necessarily be a fruitless one. Yet hereditarian social attitudes are still part of our social fabric and they remain a context for the findings of that research. In the end, the responsibility for how those findings are understood and used in policy decisions will be in the hands of scientists and educators alike. We will have to critically analyze the forces of material and intellectual determinism that would limit the lives of today's young people. In that way we will fulfill our responsibility as professionals and citizens while responding to the concerns of those who fear for eugenics' return. Through such a combination of critical scientific understanding, historical awareness, and social vision, we can resist the capturing of science for political ends. One can also hope that through a deepened understanding of the history of eugenics and American education and through a cautious approach to the contemporary study of markers and complex human behavior we can be as sure as our postmodern world will allow that the past need not be prologue.

While it is certainly true that American eugenicists actively sought a role in American policymaking in the period between the turn of the century and the 1940s, it is also true that no one is a Mendelian eugenicist today. That is, no one suggests that the majority of human behaviors are caused by single genes easily under the breeder's control. As noted in the previous discussion of covariance effects, we now recognize that most complex human traits are the product of many genes acting together in an environmental context that begins at fertilization. These lifelong contexts, these environmental influences, are powerful forces that impact the growth, development, and expression of human potentialities. For educators and citizens concerned for social justice, the implications are clear. Since there are so few examples of single hereditary factors that determine complex behavior, we must turn our attention to creating maximally supportive environments for our children. Despite recurring arguments to the contrary, arguments positing that race and class are genetically driven determiners of performance and that environmental interventions are of no avail (Herrnstein & Murray, 1994; Jensen, 1969, 1981), it is in fact just the environment that is open to our modest control. Neither the race nor the class of our students suggests any a priori limitation on their possibilities. Such views, informed as they are by unfounded notions of difference, not only represent bad policy but depend on bad science as well.

Yet today there is a renewed interest in finding nonracial genetic explanations for human behavior, explanations that are surprisingly like the eugenicists' search for single determining factors. Given the history described in the previous chapters, this should not be surprising. After all, hereditarian attitudes have been a component of American social thought throughout this century. In our contemporary context, the Human Genome Project and continuing breakthroughs in medical genetics, while having no scientific link to eugenics, surely serve to reinforce those attitudes (Kevles & Hood, 1992). Of course no thoughtful person would reject the idea of heredity in human development. It is rather the idea of the determinism of inheritance, the idea of the determinism of biology, and particularly the idea that a single gene must determine complex behavior that we reject today. Except for twins, each of us is genetically unique and we understand that heredity plays a role in that uniqueness. It just does not determine our individual humanity.

But a nagging question does seem to remain—"all right, genes may not determine who we are all by themselves, but don't they play a role in influencing human behavior?" Of course they do. But attempts to measure that role are often problematic (Kamin, 1974; Kamin & Eysenck, 1981). As noted before, attempts to separate the contributions of nature and nurture, attempts to explain human behavior as combined percentages of nature-plus-nurture ("30% of her pleasant personality is caused by nature while 70% is attributable to nurture") are fruitless. Again, this empirical reality has implications for policy. Our moral responsibility for those disadvantaged by life's contingencies should not lead us to create a nature–nurture calculus and then to throw up our hands in despair that nothing can be done due to the uncontrollable determinism of nature. It is far more reasonable, and ethically appropriate, to consider the ways we live as a community, to compare that reality with a politically developed sense of social justice, and then to develop policies in line with our spirits' best angels.

But surely, given our discussion in this chapter of markers and behavior, there are levels of human performance that are significantly influenced by genetics. This is so, but we have also argued that determinist arguments are unhelpful, and in most instances wrong. What then should we do? Should we resist policies based on genetic explanations for differential human performance on their face? Should we reject them for political or ideological reasons? Of course not. Our task is to evaluate the data; when unwarranted genetic evidence is offered it must be rejected. But care must be taken here since we have to work at two levels simultaneously. We must focus on the quality of the genetic justification for our policies, while at the same time evaluating the ethical worth of the programs themselves (Scheffler, 1968).

Here the historical links between a belief in racial distinctions and U.S. policies of immigration restriction may serve as a useful example. Regardless of one's position on immigration early in this century, one could not justify closing America's doors on genetic grounds. In the 1920s there was no evidence that certain ethnic groups were inherently less able than others. There is no such evidence today. Of course humankind is varied, but there is no scientific support for a belief in the existence of racial hierarchies. Further, there is no scientific evidence that persons of differing ethnic backgrounds will make differential contributions to America, based on their ethnicity.

The point here is particularly relevant for educators concerned with the issues of ethnic differences and the evaluation of differential school performance. Our history tells us that attributing these differences to race is profoundly dangerous, and most importantly, scientifically unjustified. Educational testing programs that take cognizance of human differences, a fact that no one disputes, are appropriate. But they should be directed toward students' possibilities, not their limitations. Such programs should be directed toward increasing routes to access, to facilitating that which students can do. That is to say, they should be used as a diagnostic tool. They should not be used to measure and categorize students in order to segregate and diminish their opportunities. It was toward diagnosis, we should remember, that Alfred Binet developed his original French examination programs. That these diagnostic instruments became intellectual Procrustean beds when transferred to an American context should be of no small moment for today's policymakers and citizens. If many today support policies of testing for diagnosis, we should recognize that it is as a consequence of hard-fought battles. Given today's national obsession with testing for comparative purposes, we would be wise to remember Binet's original intentions.

Our study of the history of American Eugenics also raises the issue of resource allocation to individuals having specific identifiable genetic conditions. Consider the example of persons with Down Syndrome. Down Syndrome is a genetic fact of life, but by itself it says nothing about social policy. Those who recommend policies of segregation and institutionalization might argue that children with this condition do not deserve access to public education or the benefit of publicly funded social services. I would disagree. As Louise Reynolds (personal communication, August 1997) points out, "even though Down Syndrome is a readily identifiable genetic anomaly, there is a wide range of abilities that need to be nurtured in order for individuals to meet their full potential." One need only compare the effects of the institutionalization of Down Syndrome children a generation ago with the consequences of today's programs of early intervention and therapy to recognize Reynolds's point. Today, thanks to these contemporary policies, many of these individuals live "reasonably independent lives and are productive and contributing members of their society. This wasn't the case with the previous generation, who were rarely given the opportunity to reach their developmental potential." The point here is that our scientific understanding of individuals with Down Syndrome has not changed; our policy has. Our ethical positions, unlike our scientific knowledge, do not arise from an analysis of chromosomes; they result from discussions of competing goods. Scientific knowledge does not prefigure ethics. Policy decisions are not driven by our biological understanding in these cases; they are informed by them. As Reynolds points out, Michael Meaney's (1994) work might shed useful light on "how early intervention programs might allow for the increase in neural function that allows potential to increase at an earlier age." But these data require a policy for their translation into practice. A reasonable educational policy should include meeting individuals' needs, maximizing potential, and increasing social inclusion. Such a policy applies to all children. It is important that we recognize that the values of inclusion, community, and the development of potential are not biological categories. Social justice is not to be derived from the facts of the biological world. Biological data are not the engines of policymaking; they are important components of that deliberative process.

In the previous example of policy formation, the biological evidence was substantial. But care must be taken that we not use unwarranted genetic explanations as we argue for worthy programs and benign ends. Here we might reflect on our earlier discussion of the limited evidence of the role genetics plays in sexual orientation. The caution here is that the political goal of validating a range of sexual orientations including homosexuality is not strengthened when it is based on unjustified evidence. In the long run, such approaches are likely to fail, leaving the proponents of the worthy goal at risk. Talk of a "gay gene," even when it is viewed as a corrective to cultural ignorance and destructive homophobic behavior, is meaningless. Genes do not produce behavior. Genes produce enzymes and enzymes control chemical processes. The search for social legitimacy can more easily be found in political and ethical discourse than in genetics.

While some in the community choose to use genetics for political purposes, others reject genetic explanations on historical grounds. I would counsel caution here. The motivation to reject comes from the recognition that many of this century's most destructive acts were justified in terms of eugenics. But the realization that eugenics had been used to justify the most odious of ends should not lead us to take a priori positions against genetic explanations for human behavior. The Holocaust was not an expression of genetics; it was among other things the application of eugenic policies to ends so awful that it is recognized as unique in human history. And indeed what was true in the 1930s is still true today—racist and nativist arguments have no scientific standing. To despair in the face of the Holocaust is justified. And the rejection of eugenics as bad science is equally well founded. Yet neither of these positions logically leads to the rejection of the science of human genetics.

Determinist arguments, as I noted at the beginning of this volume, are at least as old as ancient Athens and the work of Plato. Over four centuries ago these very same arguments vexed Shakespeare, who stood against determinism as he had his problematic character Cassius instruct that the responsibility for our behavior lies "not in our stars but in ourselves" (*Julius Caesar*, act I, scene 2). Shakespeare was right of course. Neither our stars in the 16th century nor our genes in the 20th prefigure human complexity or social justice. We must take responsibility for our actions. This is not a recommendation that we reject science. On the contrary, we must understand that "we will never get very far in either moral or scientific inquiries if we disregard facts because we do not like their implications" (Gould, 1998). But as we have seen in the preceding chapters, when American Mendelian eugenics was linked to American educational policy, neither science nor morality was much in evidence. Of the many lessons we learn from this historical rendering of eugenics, two appear to stand out. In our complex world, we must learn to parse both the scientific and the ethical realities that confront us. To put this another way, we must understand as well as take responsibility for our world. These are neither the requirements of our stars nor of our genes. In the final analysis they are the requirements of our humanity.

References

Allen, G. (1986). The Eugenics Record Office at Cold Spring Harbor, 1910–1940: An essay on institutional history. *OSIRIS, 2nd Series, 2,* 225–264.

Allen, G., & Futterman, A. (1995). *The biological basis of crime: An historical and methodological study.* Paper presented before the Meaning and Significance of Claims of Genetic Influence on Criminal Behavior Conference's section on the historical and social contexts of genetic explanations of criminal behavior, University of Maryland, College Park.

Angier, N. (1993, October 22). Study finds a genetic flaw that may explain some male violence. *New York Times,* p. A10.

Angier, N. (1996, January 2). Variant gene tied to love of new thrills. *New York Times,* p. A1.

Apple, M. W. (1986). *Teachers and texts.* New York: Routledge & Kegan Paul.

Bagley, W. C. (1911). *Educational values.* New York: Macmillan.

Bagley, W. C. (1922). Professor Terman's determinism: A rejoinder. *Journal of Educational Research, 6,* 371–385.

Bagley, W. C. (1925). *Determinism in education.* Baltimore: Warwick and York.

Begley, S. (1996, January 15). Holes in those genes: Not even DNA can live up to all the hyped claims. *Newsweek,* p. 57.

Bigelow, M. A. (1946). Brief history of the American Eugenics Society. *Eugenical News, 31,* 49–51.

Billings, P. R., Beckwith, J., & Alper, J. S. (1992). The genetic analysis of human behavior: A new era? *Social Science & Medicine, 35,* 227–238.

Blum, K., Noble, E. P., Sheridan, P. J., Montgomery, A., Ritchie, T., Jagaderswaran, P., Nogami, H., Briggs, A. H., & Cohn, J. B. (1990). Allelic association of human dopamine D2 receptor gene in alcoholism. *Journal of the American Medical Association, 263,* 2055–2060.

Bobbitt, J. F. (1909). Practical eugenics. *Pedagogical Seminary, 16,* 385–394.

Bobbitt, J. F. (1918). *The curriculum.* Boston: Houghton-Mifflin Company.

Borogoankar, D. S., & Shah, S. A. (1974). The XYY chromosome male—or syndrome? *Progress in Medical Genetics, 10,* 135–222.

Brigham, C. C. (1923). *A study of American intelligence.* Princeton, NJ: Princeton University Press.

Brigham, C. C. (1930). Intelligence tests of immigrant groups. *Psychological Review, 37,* 158–165.

Brooks-Dunn, J., Klebanov, P. K., & Guncan, G. J. (1996). Ethnic differences in childrens intelligence test scores: Role of economic deprivation, home environment, and maternal characteristics. *Child Development, 67,* 396–408.

Bouchard, T. J., Jr., Lykken, D. T., McGue, M., Segal, N. L., & Tellegan, A. (1989). Sources of human psychological differences: The Minnesota twin study of twins reared apart. *Science, 250,* 223–228.

Boydston, J. A. (Ed.). (1977). *John Dewey: The middle works, 1899–1924,* Volume 4, 1907–1909. Carbondale: Southern Illinois University Press.

Buck v. Bell. (1927). 274 U.S. 200, 47 S. Ct. 584.

Byne, W. (1994, May). The biological evidence challenged. *Scientific American,* pp. 50–55.

Campbell, C. G. (1929). Euthenics and eugenics. *Eugenics, 3*(9), 3–5.

Chase, A. (1977). *The legacy of Malthus: The social costs of the new scientific racism.* New York: Alfred A. Knopf.

Cicchetti, D., & Beeghly, M. (Eds.). (1990). *Children with Down Syndrome: A developmental perspective.* New York: Cambridge University Press.

Conklin, E. G. (1923). *Heredity and environment in the development of man* (3rd ed.). Princeton, NJ: Princeton University Press.

Conn, H. W. (1914). *Social heredity and social evolution: The other side of eugenics.* New York: Abingdon Press.

Cowan, R. S. (1969). *Sir Francis Galton and the study of heredity in the nineteenth century.* Unpublished doctoral dissertation, The Johns Hopkins University, Baltimore.

Cox, E. S. (1923). *White America.* Richmond: White American Society.

Cravens, H. (1978). *The triumph of evolution: American scientists and the heredity-environment controversy, 1900–1941.* Philadelphia: University of Pennsylvania Press.

Curti, M. (1959). The social ideas of American educators. Ottawa: Littlefield Adams. (Original work published 1935)

Cutten, G. B. (1922). The reconstruction of democracy. *School and Society, 16,* 477–489.

Davenport, C. B. (1911). *Heredity in relation to eugenics.* New York: Henry Holt.

Davenport, C. B. (1913). *Eugenics record office bulletin No. 9: State laws limiting marriage selection in light of eugenics.* Cold Spring Harbor, NY: Eugenics Record Office.

Davenport, C. B. (Ed.). (1923a). *Eugenics, genetics, and the family: Vol. I. Scientific papers of the second international congress of eugenics.* Baltimore: Williams and Wilkins.

Davenport, C. B. (Ed.). (1923b). *Eugenics in race and state: Vol. II. Scientific papers of the second international congress of eugenics.* Baltimore: Williams and Wilkins.

Davenport, C. B. (1934). Presidential address: The development of eugenics. In H. F. Perkins (Ed.), *A decade of progress in eugenics: Scientific papers of the third international congress of eugenics* (pp. 17–22). Baltimore: The Williams & Wilkins Company.

Dawidowicz, L. S. (1975). *The war against the Jews.* New York: Holt, Rinehart and Winston.

Dewey, J. (1909). Address to the National Negro Conference 1909. *Proceedings of the National Negro Conference 1909* (pp. 71–73). New York: National Negro Conference Headquarters.

Dewey, J. (1922, December 6). Mediocrity and individuality. *The New Republic,* pp. 35–37.

Dobzhansky, T., & Montagu, M. F. (1947). Natural selection and the mental capacities of mankind. *Science, 105,* 587–590.

Dunn, L. C. (Ed.). (1951). *Genetics in the twentieth century.* New York: Macmillan.

Elson, R. M. (1964). *Guardians of tradition: American schoolbooks of the nineteenth century.* Lincoln: University of Nebraska Press.

Eugenical News, 9. (1924, January). Cold Spring Harbor, NY: The Eugenics Research Association and the Eugenics Society of the United States of America.

Eugenical News, 10. (1925, February). Cold Spring Harbor, NY: The Eugenics Research Association and the Eugenics Society of the United States of America.

Eugenical News, 13. (1928, February). Cold Spring Harbor, NY: The Eugenics Research Association and the Eugenics Society of the United States of America.

Eugenical News, 16. (1931, January). Cold Spring Harbor, NY: The Eugenics Research Association and the Eugenics Society of the United States of America.

Eugenics: A journal of race betterment, Volume IV, Number 1 (December 1931). New Haven: The American Eugenics Society.

Evans, W. S. (1931). *Organized eugenics.* New Haven: American Eugenics Society.

Fancher, R. E. (1985). *The intelligence men: Makers of the I.Q. controversy.* New York: W. W. Norton.

Fisher, I. (1915). Eugenics—Foremost plan of human redemption. *Official Proceedings: Volume II, proceedings of the second national conference on race betterment.* Battle Creek: The Race Betterment Foundation.

Freeman, D. M. (1929, July 13). Criteria for judging a science of education. *School and Society.*

Galton, F. (1883). *Inquiries into human faculty and its development.* London: J. M. Dent and Sons.

Goddard, H. H. (1912). *The Kallikak family: A study in the heredity of feeble-mindedness.* New York: Macmillan.

Goddard, H. H. (1924). Bridging the gap between our knowledge of child well-being and our care of the young. In M. V. O'Shea (Ed.), *The child: His nature and his needs* (pp. 159–175). New York: The Children's Foundation.

Gorman, C. (1995, November 13). Trapped in the body of a man? *Time,* pp. 94–95.

Gottesman, I., & Goldsmith, H. H. (in press). Developmental psychopathology of antisocial behavior: Inserting genes into its ontogenesis and epigenesis. In C. A. Nelson (Ed.), *Threats to optimal development: Integrating biological, psychological, and social risk factors.*

Gould, S. J. (1980). Dr. Down's Syndrome. In S. J. Gould (Ed.), *The panda's thumb: More reflections on natural history* (pp. 160–168). New York: W. W. Norton & Company.

Gould, S. J. (1981). *The mismeasure of man.* New York: W. W. Norton.

Gould, S. J. (1987). Carrie Buck's daughter. In S. J. Gould (Ed.), *The flamingo's smile: reflections on natural history* (pp. 306–318). New York: W. W. Norton.

Gould, S. J. (1993). Cordelia's dilemma. *Natural History, 107*(2), 22–78.

Gould, S. J. (1996, February 22). Thrill of sliding goes straight to the bone. *New York Times,* p. B15.

Gould, S. J. (1998). The internal brand of the scarlet. W. *Natural History, 102*(2), 10–18.

Graham, L. R. (1978). Attitudes towards eugenics in Germany and Soviet Russia in the 1920s: An examination of science and values. In H. T. Englehardt, Jr., & D. Callahan (Eds.), *Morals, science and society, Vol. III: The foundations of ethics and its relationship to science* (pp. 119–149). Hastings-on-Hudson, NY: The Hastings Center Institute of Society, Ethics, and Life Sciences.

Graham, P. A. (1991, January). *What America has expected from its schools over the past century.* Paper presented at the Benton Center for Curriculum and Instruction, Conference on Democracy and Education, University of Chicago, Illinois.

Grant, M. (1921). *The passing of the great race or the racial basis of European history.* New York: Charles Scribners & Sons.

Gregory, W. (1919). Letter dated April 1919. Henry Fairfield Osborn Files, American Museum of Natural History.

Gregory, W. (1922). Letter dated October 11, 1922. Henry Fairfield Osborn Papers, American Museum of Natural History.

Gregory, W. (1930). Letter dated October 20, 1930. Henry Fairfield Osborn Papers, American Museum of Natural History.

Guyer, M. F. (1916). *Being well-born: An introduction to eugenics.* Indianapolis: Bobbs-Merrill.

Guyer, M. F. (1948). *Animal biology* (4th ed.). New York: Harper Brothers.

Haller, M. H. (1963). *Eugenics: Hereditarian attitudes in American thought.* New Brunswick, NJ: Rutgers University Press.

Hamer, D., Hu, S., Magnuson, V., Hu, N., & Pattatucci, A. M. (1993). A linkage between DNA markers on the X chromosome and male sexual orientation. *Science, 261,* 321–327.

Herrnstein, R. J., & Murray, C. (1994). *The bell curve: Intelligence and class structure in American life.* Boston: The Free Press.

Higham, J. (1974). *Strangers in the land: Patterns of American nativism, 1860–1925.* New York: Atheneum.

Hodson, C. B. (1929). Feminism and the race. *Eugenics, 2*(12), 1–3.

Hollingworth, L. S. (1924). Provisions for intellectually superior children. In M. V. O'Shea (Ed.), *The child: His nature and his needs* (pp. 277–299). New York: The Children's Foundation.

Hollingworth, L. S. (1926). *Gifted children: Their nature and nurture.* New York: Macmillan.

Hollingworth, L. S. (1929). The production of gifted children from the parental point of view. *Eugenics, 2*(10), pp. 3–7.

Hunter, G. W. (1914). *A civic biology: Presented in problems.* New York: American Book Company.

Hunter, G. W. (1926). *New civic biology: Presented in problems.* New York: American Book Company.

Hunter, G. W. (1931). *Problems in biology.* New York: American Book Company.

Hunter, G. W. (1941). *Life science: A social biology.* New York: American Book Company.

Hunter, G. W., & Whitman, W. G. (1935). *Science in our world of progress.* New York: American Book Company.

Husen, T. (1984). Research and policy making in education: An international perspective. *Educational Researcher, 13,* 5–11.

Ireland, A. (1923). The nature-nurture issue in its bearing upon government. In C. B. Davenport (Ed.), *Eugenics in race and state: Vol. II. Scientific papers of the second international conference of eugenics* (pp. 419–426). Baltimore: Williams and Wilkins.

Jacobs, P. A., Brunton, M., Melville, M. M., Brittain, R. P., & McClement, W. F. (1965). Aggressive behavior, mental subnormality and the xyy male. *Nature, 208*, 1351–1352.

Janik, A., & Toulmin, S. (1973). *Wittgenstein's Vienna.* New York: Simon and Schuster.

Jennings, H. S. (1930). *The biological basis of human nature.* New York: W. W. Norton.

Jensen, A. R. (1969). How much can we boost IQ and scholastic achievement? *Harvard Educational Review, 39*(1), 1–123.

Jensen, A. R. (1981). *Straight talk about mental tests.* New York: Macmillan.

Kaback, M. M., Rimoink, D. L., & O'Brien, J. S. (Eds.). (1977). Tay-Sachs disease, screening and prevention. New York: A. R. Liss.

Kagen, J. (1993). *Unstable ideas: Temperament, cognition and self.* Cambridge: Harvard University Press.

Kamin, L. (1974). *The science and politics of I.Q.* New York: John Wiley & Sons.

Kamin, L. (1993, December). The temper of the times. *Readings: A Journal of Reviews and Commentary in Mental Health,* pp. 4–7.

Kamin, L., & Eysenck, H. (1981). *The intelligence controversy.* New York: John Wiley & Sons.

Kellogg, J. H. (1914). Needed—A new human race. In E. F. Robbins (Ed.), *Official proceedings: Vol. I, Proceedings of the first national conference on race betterment* (pp. 431–450). Battle Creek, MI: The Race Betterment Foundation.

Kellogg, J. H. (1915). The eugenics registry. In *Official proceedings: Vol. II, Proceedings of the second national conference on race betterment.* Battle Creek, MI: The Race Betterment Foundation.

Kellogg, J. H. (1929). Medicine and race betterment: Do their doctrines conflict? *Eugenics, 2*(6).

Kevles, D. (1985). *In the name of eugenics: Genetics and the uses of human heredity.* New York: Alfred A. Knopf.

Kevles, D., & Hood, L. (1992). *The code of codes: Scientific and social issues in the human genome project.* Cambridge: Harvard University Press.

Key, W. E. (1923). Heritable factors in human fitness and their social control. In C. B. Davenport (Ed.), *Eugenics, genetics, and the family: Vol. I. Scientific papers of the second international congress of eugenics* (pp. 405–412). Baltimore: Williams and Wilkins.

Kliebard, H. M. (1986). *The struggle for the American curriculum, 1893–1959.* Boston: Routledge & Kegan Paul.

Kolata, G. A. (1997, February 24). With cloning of a sheep, the ethical ground shifts. *New York Times,* p. A1.

Laughlin, H. H. (1929). The progress of eugenics. *Eugenics, 2*(2), 3–15.

LeVay, S., & Hamer, D. (1994, May). Evidence for a biological influence in male homosexuality. *Scientific American,* pp. 44–49.

Lippmann, W. (1922a, November 29). A future for the tests. *The New Republic,* pp. 9–10.

Lippmann, W. (1922b, October 25). The mental age of Americans. *The New Republic*, pp. 213–215.

Lippmann, W. (1922c, November 8). The reliability of intelligence tests. *The New Republic*, pp. 275–277.

Lippmann, W. (1922d, November 22). Tests of hereditary intelligence. *The New Republic*, pp. 328–330.

Little, C. C. (1928a). *Proceedings of the Third Race Betterment Conference, January 2–6, 1928*. Battle Creek, MI: The Race Betterment Foundation.

Little, C. C. (1928b). The relation of eugenics to education. *Eugenics, 1*(1), pp. 1–3.

Lombardo, P. A. (1985). Three generations, no imbeciles: New light on Buck v. Bell. *New York University Law Review, 60*, 30–62.

Loving v. Virginia (1967). 388 U.S. 1.

Ludmerer, K. M. (1972). *Genetics and American society: A historical appraisal*. Baltimore: Johns Hopkins Press.

Mackenzie, D. A. (1981). *Statistics in Britain, 1865–1930: The social construction of scientific knowledge*. Edinburgh: Edinburgh University Press.

Mayr, E. (1982). *The growth of biological thought: Diversity, evolution, and inheritance*. Cambridge: Harvard University Press.

Meaney, M. J. (1994). Early environmental programming: Hypothalmic-pituitary-adrenal responses to stress. *Seminars in the Neurosciences, 6*, 247–259.

Miller, H. A. (1914). The psychological limits of eugenics. In E. F. Robbins (Ed.), *Official proceedings: Vol. I, proceedings of the first national conference on race betterment* (pp. 464–471). Battle Creek, MI: Race Betterment Foundation.

Mjoen, J. A. (1923). Harmonic and disharmonic race crossings. In C. B. Davenport (Ed.), *Eugenics in race and state: Vol. II. Scientific papers of the second international congress of eugenics* (pp. 41–61). Baltimore: Williams and Wilkins.

Mjoen, J. A. (1930). The masculine education of women and its dangers. *Eugenics, 3*(9), 323–326.

Montagu, M. F. A. (1942). *Man's most dangerous myth: The fallacy of race*. New York: Columbia University Press.

Morgan, T. H., Sturtevant, A. H., Muller, H. J., & Bridges, C. B. (1915). *The mechanism of Mendelian heredity*. New York: Henry Holt.

Morrison, T. (1970). *The bluest eye*. New York: Pocket Books.

NEA Bulletin. (1917, April).

Osborn, H. F. (1928). Letter dated November 20, 1928. Henry Fairfield Osborn Papers, American Museum of Natural History.

Osborn, H. F. (1934). Birth selection versus birth control. In H. F. Perkins (Ed.), *A decade of progress in eugenics: Scientific papers of the third international congress of eugenics* (pp. 29–41). Baltimore: Williams and Wilkins.

Oskaloosa Herald. (1913, June). Goddard talks on feebleminded, p. 1.

Paul, D. (1995). *Controlling human heredity: 1865 to the present*. New Jersey: Humanities Press.

Peabody, J. E., & Hunt, A. E. (1924). *Biology and human welfare*. New York: Macmillan. (Original work published 1914).

Persons, S. (1958). *American minds: A history of ideas*. New York: Holt, Reinhart and Winston.

Peters, C. C. (1930). *Foundations of educational sociology.* New York: Macmillan.

Pickens, D. K. (1963). *Eugenics and the progressives.* Nashville, TN: Vanderbuilt University Press.

Plomin, R. (1990). The role of inheritance in behavior. *Science, 248,* 183–188.

Plomin, R., Owen, M., & McGuffin, P. (1994). The genetic basis of complex human behaviors. *Science, 264,* 1733–1739.

Popenoe, P. (1915). Natural selection in man. *Official Proceedings: Vol. II, Official Proceedings of the Second National Conference on Race Betterment.* Battle Creek, MI: The Race Betterment Foundation.

Popenoe, P., & Johnson, R. (1918). *Applied eugenics.* New York: Macmillan.

Popenoe, P., & Johnson, R. (1935). *Applied eugenics: Third edition.* New York: Macmillan.

Provine, W. B. (1971). *The origins of theoretical population genetics.* Chicago and London: The University of Chicago Press.

Punnett, R. C. (1912). Genetics and eugenics [Abstract]. *Problems in Eugenics: Papers communicated to the First International Eugenics Congress* (pp. 137–138). London: The Eugenics Education Society.

Punnett, R. C. (1917). Eliminating feeblemindedness. *Journal of Heredity,* 464–465.

Putnam, H. C. (1916). The new ideal in education—Better parents of better children. In *Addresses and Proceedings of the National Education Association, 54,* (pp. 240–245). Ann Arbor, MI: National Education Association.

Putnam, H. C. (1921). Second report of progress of Committee on Racial Well-Being. *Addresses and Proceedings of the National Education Association, 59,* 362. Washington, DC: National Education Association.

Putnam, H. C. (1922). Report of the Committee on Racial Well-Being. *Addresses and Proceedings of the National Education Association, 60,* 562–564. Washington, DC: National Education Association.

Race Betterment Foundation. (1915). Natural selection in man. *Official proceedings of the second national conference on race betterment.* Battle Creek, MI.

Reich, T. (1998). Biologic-marker studies in alcoholism. *New England Journal of Medicine, 318,* 180–182.

Riis, J. A. (1914). The bad boy. In E. F. Robbins (Ed.), *Official Proceedings: Vol. I, Proceedings of the first national conference on race betterment* (pp. 241–250). Battle Creek, MI: Race Betterment Foundation.

Ripley, W. Z. (1899). *The races of Europe.* London: Routledge, Paul, Trench, Trubner & Co.

Risch, N., Squires-Wheeler, E., & Keats, B. J. (1993). Male sexual orientation and genetic evidence. *Science, 262,* 2063–2065.

Ritchie, J. W. (1941). *Biology in human affairs.* New York: World Book Company.

Rose, S. (1995, February). The rise of neurogenetic determinism. *Nature, 373,* 380–382.

Rosenberg, C. E. (1961). *No other gods: On science and American social thought.* Baltimore: Johns Hopkins University Press.

Rosenberg, C. E. (1974). The bitter fruit: heredity, disease, and social thought in nineteenth century America. *Perspectives in American History, 8,* 189–235.

Ross, E. A. (1904). The value rank of the American people. *The Independent, 57,* 1061–1064.

Rushton, J. P. (1988). Race differences in behaviour: A review and evolutionary analysis. *Personality and Individual Differences, 9,* 1009–1024.

Rutherford, J. F. (1989). *Project 2061: Science for all Americans.* Washington, DC: American Association for the Advancement of Science.

Sadler, L. K. (1934). Is the abnormal to become the normal? In H. F. Perkins (Ed.), *A decade of progress in eugenics: Scientific papers of the Third International Congress of Eugenics* (pp. 193–200). Baltimore: Williams and Wilkins.

Scheffler, I. (1968). *The language of education.* Springfield: Charles Thomas.

Selden, S. (1978). Eugenics and curriculum: Conservative naturalism in education, 1860–1929. *The Educational Forum, 43*(1), 67–82.

Selden, S. (1983). Biological determinism and the roots of student classification. *Journal of Education, 165*(2), 175–191.

Selden, S. (1984). Objectivity and ideology in educational research. *Phi Delta Kappan, 66*(4), 181–183.

Selden, S. (1985). Education policy and biological science: Genetics, eugenics, and the college textbook, c. 1908–1931. *Teachers College Record, 87*(1), 35–52.

Selden, S. (1987). Professionalism and the null curriculum: The case of the popular eugenics movement and American educational studies. *Educational Studies, 18,* 221–238.

Selden, S. (1988a). Biological determinism and the normal school curriculum: Helen Putnam and the NEA Committee on Racial Well-Being, 1910–1922. In W. Pinar (Ed.), *Contemporary curriculum discourses* (pp. 50–65). Scottsdale: Gorsuch Scarisbrick, Publishers.

Selden, S. (1988b). Resistance in school and society: Public and pedagogical debates about eugenics, 1900–1947. *Teachers College Record, 90*(1), 61–84.

Selden, S. (1989). The use of biology to legitimate inequality: The eugenics movement within the high school biology textbook, 1914–1949. In W. Secada (Ed.), *Equity in Education* (pp. 118–145). New York: The Falmer Press.

Selden, S. (1994, Fall). Early twentieth century biological determinism and the classification of exceptional students. In G. Macdonald (Ed.), *Evaluation and Research in Education.* North Somerset: Multilingual Matters Ltd.

Sherborn, F. B. (1934). *The child: His origin, development and care.* New York: McGraw-Hill.

Shultze, A. H. (1923). Plate 11, Comparison of white and Negro fetuses. In H. H. Laughlin (Secretary), *Eugenics in Race and State: Vol. II. Scientific papers of the Second International Congress of Eugenics.* Baltimore: Williams and Wilkins.

Smith, D. J., & Nelson, K. R. (1989). *The sterilization of Carrie Buck.* Far Hills, NJ: New Horizons Press.

Smith, G. F. (Ed.). (1985). *Molecular structure of the Number 21 Chromosome and Down syndrome.* New York: New York Academy of Sciences.

Snedden, D. (1931). When wives go to business: Is it eugenically helpful? *Eugenics, 4*(1), 19–20.

Spencer, H. (1914). In E. F. Robbins (Ed.), *Proceedings of the First Race National Conference on Race Betterment* (title page). Battle Creek, MI: Race Betterment Foundation.

Steggerda, M. (1944). Dr. Charles B. Davenport and his contributions to eugenics. *Eugenical News, 29*, 3–7.

Stoddard, L. (1920). *The rising tide of color against white world supremacy.* New York: Charles Scribner's Sons.

Tait, W. D. (1925). Psychology, education and sociology. *School and Society, 21*, 33–37.

Thorndike, R. L. (1931). *Human learning.* New York: The Century Co.

United States Supreme Court Records, 1927, p. 207.

Ward, R. D. (1914). Race betterment and our immigration laws. In E. F. Robbins (Ed.), *Official Proceedings: Vol. I, Proceedings of the First National Conference on Race Betterment* (pp. 542–546). Battle Creek, MI: Race Betterment Foundation.

Washington, B. T. (1914). The Negro race. In E. F. Robbins (Ed.), *Official Proceedings: Vol. I, Proceedings of the First National Conference on Race Betterment* (pp. 410–420). Battle Creek, MI: Race Betterment Foundation.

Wasserman, D. (1996). Research into genetics and crime: Consensus and controversy. *Political and Life Sciences, 15*, 107–109.

West, L. S. (1928). The practical application of eugenic principles. In C. C. Little (Ed.), *Official Proceedings, Vol. III: Proceedings of the Third National Conference on Race Betterment* (pp. 91–117). Battle Creek, MI: The Race Betterment Foundation.

Wexler, N. (1992). Clairvoyance and caution: Repercussions from the Human Genome Project. In D. Kelves & L. Hood (Eds.), *The code of codes: Scientific issues in the Human Genome Project* (pp. 211–243). Cambridge: Harvard University Press.

Wheeler, D. L. (1992, June 24). An escalating debate over research that links biology and human behavior. *The Chronicle of Higher Education*, p. A7.

Whipple, G. M. (1928). *National society for the study of education, twenty-seventh yearbook, nature and nurture, part 1, their influence on intelligence.* Bloomington: National Society for the Study of Education.

Wiggam, A. E. (1922). *The new decalogue of science.* New York: Bobbs-Merrill Company.

Woods, F. A. (1923). The conification of social groups: Evidence from New England families. In C. B. Davenport (Chair), *Eugenics, genetics, and the family: Vol. I. Scientific Papers of the Second International Congress of Eugenics* (pp. 312–328). Baltimore: Williams and Wilkins.

Yerkes, R. M. (1916). Educational and psychological aspects of racial well-being. In *Addresses and Proceedings of the National Education Association, 54* (pp. 248–252). Ann Arbor, MI: National Education Association.

Index

About the Author

Professor Steven Selden received his doctorate from Teachers College, Columbia University in 1971. He is currently Program Coordinator of the Curriculum Theory and Development Program at the University of Maryland at College Park. He received a Fulbright Lectureship at the Beijing Normal University in the People's Republic of China in 1994 and is the recipient of the University of Maryland's College of Education's Outstanding Faculty Award and the Education Press Association of America's Distinguished Achievement Award for Excellence in Educational Journalism.